Second Language Acquisition

General Editors: Paul Meara and Peter Skehan

Also available in this series:
Theories of Second-Language Learning
Barry McLaughlin

Variation in Interlanguage
Elaine Tarone

Individual Differences in Second-Language Learning

Peter Skehan

Lecturer in Education, Institute of Education, University of London

Edward Arnold
A division of Hodder & Stoughton
LONDON NEW YORK MELBOURNE AUCKLAND

© 1989 Peter Skehan

First published in Great Britain 1989

Distributed in the USA by Routledge, Chapman and Hall, Inc.
29 West 35th Street, New York, NY 10001

British Library Cataloguing in Publication Data

Skehan, Peter
   Individual differences in second-language learning-
   (Second language acquisition).
   1. Foreign languages. Learning
   I. Title   II. Series
   418′.007

   ISBN 0–7131–6602–9

Library of Congress Cataloging-in-Publication Data

Skehan, Peter.
   Individual differences in second-language learning.
   (Second language acquisition)
   Bibliography: p.
   Includes index.
   1. Second language acquisition.   2. Individual differences.
I. Title. II. Series.
P118.2.S57 1989   418′.007   88-33351
ISBN 0–7131–6602–9

Typeset in 10/11 pt English Times by Colset Private Limited,
Singapore
Printed and bound in Great Britain for Edward Arnold, the
educational, academic and medical publishing division of Hodder
and Stoughton Limited, 41 Bedford Square, London WC1B 3DQ
by Richard Clay plc, Bungay Suffolk

Contents

Acknowledgements

I would never have written this book without the inspiration of two researchers who have contributed fundamental work on the role of individual differences in language learning – Jack Carroll and Robert Gardner. It was they who made me realise how important the field is. I am also very grateful for the help given me by Paul Meara, who edited this book. He was encouraging and constructive at all stages. I am very grateful to Richard Clement, Barry McLaughlin, and Mike Long, who each supplied very useful material on which I have drawn extensively, in the areas of motivation, interaction effects, and theory construction respectively. Finally, there are Jill, Anna, Gareth, and Daniel, who put up with a great deal during the writing of the book.

1

Theoretical foundations

In the past fifteen to twenty years, the field of second language acquisition has grown enormously, with the quantity of published research increasing annually. As a result, the accumulation of data is expanding our understanding of the complexity and range of the task of the second language learner, and so providing a sounder basis for theory construction. It is striking, however, that the main thrust of this research has been towards establishing how learners are *similar*, and what processes of learning are *universal*. Studies of universal grammar or of acquisitional sequences, or of error types, are good examples of this. Such studies are not misguided – in fact, it is research activity in areas such as those just mentioned which has brought about the increased impact of SLA research. There are, however, alternative research traditions, and it is one of these, the study of the *differences* between learners, that will be the major focus for this book.

Although the contrast between the study of common processes and the study of individual differences (IDs) is well established in other disciplines, such as psychology, this is not the case in second language learning, where a robust ID tradition is somewhat lacking. It is the aim of this book to review such ID research as exists, and to demonstrate its relevance to other aspects of SLA, so that its influence may be all the greater in the future. Chapters will try to set out the major areas in which language learners differ, covering areas such as language aptitude, motivation and cognitive style, and of individual control over learning (strategic influences). These chapters represent the main part of the book, since there is relevant (and growing) research in each area. In addition, there is coverage of the small but important area of inter-action-effects, of studies which *assume* individual differences but which then go on to examine whether particular types of individual do well when matched with particular instructional conditions. Before we approach these substantive areas though, we need, at the outset, to consider what sort of theoretical framework is appropriate for the study of Individual Differences.

Models of SLA

Model-making has been a growth area in second language learning in recent years. We shall consider four contemporary models in this chapter, and evaluate their usefulness for ID research.

The 'Language Two' or 'Monitor' model:
Dulay, Burt and Krashen (1982) propose the following model:

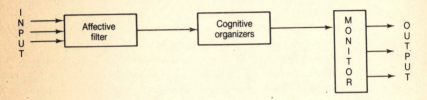

Figure 1.1: The Dulay-Burt-Krashen model

Building on this work, Krashen (1985) links the model to five hypotheses for SLA:

1 The Acquisition–Learning Hypothesis
2 The Natural Sequence Hypothesis
3 The Monitor Hypothesis
4 The Affective Filter Hypothesis
5 The Comprehensible Input Hypothesis

The 'Monitor Model' outlined above will not be discussed extensively here (see McLaughlin 1987 for a very thorough evaluation) but only as it relates to individual differences. Krashen is really proposing three general areas where variation is important. First, there is the quantity of comprehensible input. Progress is seen to be a function of the amount of such input as is available. This source of variation is outside the learner, and indeed, environmentally determined. The second source of variation is the Affective Filter. Krashen suggests that this may be raised or lowered, i.e. the learner's openness or lack of anxiety may vary, and that the 'position' of the filter will influence how much input is 'let through'. This is, potentially, an important ID involving the learner. Finally, there is variability in Monitor use. Krashen speaks of Monitor 'over-users' (those whose constant striving for correctness inhibits output), and 'under-users', (those whose lack of concern with correctness leads to garrulous but less grammatical performance).

In other words, several components in the model *could* be the source of individual differences. However, the central component, the Cognitive Organizers, is not so affected. Here, where actual 'acquisition' takes place, where Natural Sequences are preordained, where learning is irrelevant, there is only room for universal processes and *lack* of individual differences. The assumption is being made that, given comparable input, all learners will process the data in the same way and at the same speed. How much input gets through to this part of the model may vary, but the processes that operate on the input will be the same.

In fact, even those components of the Monitor Model which *seem* to be the source of IDs are disappointing when one examines them in more detail. The Monitor itself, as we have seen, appears to allow variable performance. However, Skehan (1984a) has criticized the status of the Monitor in relation to the rest of the model, suggesting that while it is concerned with on-the-spot performance, the rest of the model is concerned with the process of learning over extended time. This separation reflects the acquisition–learning distinction (Krashen 1981) in that Monitoring, being the *product* of learning, does not influence acquisition, i.e. the *process* of change. But the separation, and the postulated imperviousness of acquisition to effects of learning, means that the IDs that may exist in amount of Monitor use (i.e. 'over' and 'under' users) do not connect up with other, more central aspects of the model. To allow this to happen learning would be having an indirect effect, and the model would be self-contradictory. Since such an influence is then not permissible, IDs become trivial.

The discussion of differences elsewhere is similarly problematic. As far as both comprehensible input and affective filter variation are concerned McLaughlin (1987) has severely criticized Krashen for vagueness as to what is actually being varied. McLaughlin (1987) points out that Krashen does not explain how comprehensible input can be specified without circularity, and that no convincing account is given of how the Affective Filter changes level and on what basis it can be selective in its operation. Hence the impression we are left with is that labels have been attached to areas where it is known there is variation, but that the explanation of the variation is not advanced at all.

The 'Good Language Learner' model:

By way of contrast, we will next consider a model proposed by Naiman, Frohlich, Todesco, and Stern (1978) as part of the 'Good Language Learner' (GLL) study. The term 'model' is misleading, since what is really being proposed is only a taxonomy or listing. Still, even at this level, what Naiman *et al.* (1978) describe is interesting.

The diagram consists of five boxes, representing classes of variable in language learning. These may be divided into three independent

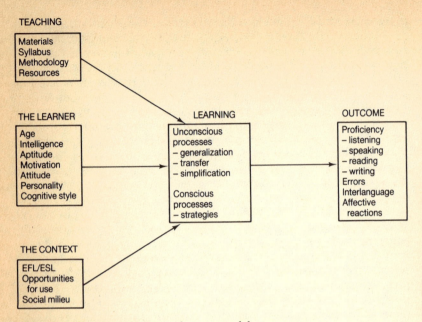

Figure 1.2: The good language-learner model

(causative) variables and two dependent (caused) variables. The independent variables, teaching, the learner, and the context, themselves have to be subdivided further, since they are each composites of many independent influences. Hence the need to specify the quality of the instruction, the quantity of resources, intelligence, personality, opportunities for informal target-language use, etc. The dependent variables also need some further subdivision. Outcome, the ultimate 'caused' variable, is seen to consist not merely of proficiency measures, but also of more qualitative aspects of performance, i.e. errors, as well as affective reactions to learning, the language, the people, and the culture concerned. The Learning box, is, perhaps, the most complex of all. It consists of two rather different things. On the one hand, there is learning, the process of developing one's competence in the target language, with the focus here being on something like Selinker's five strategies for interlanguage (Selinker 1972). On the other, there are learner strategies, which imply some degree of learner control and of distance from the actual process of learning.

The model or taxonomy shown in Figure 1.2 is essentially atheoretical, and explains very little. However it does have three advantages. First, it allows us to see the range of potential influences on language learning success. In this way, it demonstrates what varied influences there are: how difficult it is to study just one of them in isolation; how they may be classified; and what range of variables needs to be controlled in research studies. A second advantage of such a taxonomy is that, although list-based, it encourages *quantification* of the different influences. It implies that one should be able to establish how strongly aptitude or classroom organization, for example, influence the outcome of language learning: it is not enough to demonstrate 'an effect' – one must also assess how important the effect is. Finally, the GLL model offers some scope for conceptualizing interaction effects. For example, one could ask whether personality and methodology interact, with (say) extrovert learners doing particularly well in communicatively oriented classrooms, introverts doing well in teacher-led classrooms, and each learner group doing poorly when exposed to the inappropriate methodology. Since the model attempts to list the different potential influences on language learning, one has a clearer idea of where to look for interactions.

The two models outlined so far, Krashen's (Figure 1.1) and the Good Language Learner Model, (Figure 1.2) provide an interesting contrast in theory construction. McLaughlin (1987) makes a distinction between hierarchical and concatenated theories. Similarly Long (1985) and Larsen-Freeman and Long (forthcoming) distinguish between a theory-then-research approach compared to research-then-theory. The first alternative, in either case, involves the elaboration of a theory or model which makes predictions and which has explanatory power. It is (or at least should be), falsifiable, in that the predictions which are made must be capable of empirical test. The second approach suggests the identification of an area that looks promising for research and which is relatively circumscribed. The researcher then attempts to collect 'facts' in the chosen area, facts which may form a part of subsequent hierarchical theorizing.

In the present case the Monitor model would certainly be seen as a hierarchical model which operates from premises, makes predictions, and inter-relates the parts of the model in a logical system. In contrast, the Naiman model is very much in the concatenated or research-then-theory approach, providing a rudimentary categorization of relevant variables and then implying a research programme which accumulates quantitative information on the individual variables so categorized. It should enable us to reach a 'take-off' point from which it is feasible to produce more effective hierarchical theories. This is because we will have a better sight of where we are going; are less likely to ignore important data; and will have a better understanding of the scale of the problem. Certainly ID research can be conceived of much more easily within the concatenated, or research-then-theory perspective, and so the GLL model seems more appropriate as a guiding framework. This issue, though, will be returned to in Chapter 8, and pursued in the light of the intervening chapters, in which the respective strengths and weaknesses of the two approaches to theory-building will be assessed. For the present, though, two more models need to be discussed.

The Carroll model of school learning: an interactional model:
A third model to be considered is that proposed by J.B. Carroll in the early 1960s (Carroll 1965). The model was put forward to account for school learning and as a result focused on a limited set of variables. It is proposed here, however, that the model could be generalized to incorporate other variables and more complex situations. It is important that applied linguistics researchers do this, since it is argued that what are required most urgently in second language learning are models which allow both instructional (i.e. treatment) factors *and* individual difference variables to operate simultaneously.

The model, then, starts by considering two major classes of variable – instructional factors and individual difference factors. These are sub-categorized as follows:

Instructional factors
- time
- instructional excellence

Individual differences
- general intelligence
- aptitude
- motivation

The first instructional factor is time, and it is postulated that progress is a function of amount of time spent learning: the greater the time, the greater the learning. The second instructional factor is excellence of instruction. Clearly, defining instructional excellence is something of a problem, and it is striking what changes have taken place since the publication of Carroll's model in terms of what conventional wisdom now regards as good teaching. The growing field of classroom research is an attempt to at least describe classroom events and processes. For the present we will simply assume that differences in instructional effectiveness do exist, and have a place in the model.

The first of the three individual difference variables is intelligence. Carroll conceived of this as the learner's capacity to understand instruction, and to understand what is required of him in the learning situation. Intelligence, that is, is conceived of as a sort of efficiency factor, a talent for not getting sidetracked or wasting one's efforts. Aptitude, and in this case, foreign language aptitude, is seen as a generalized capacity to learn languages which is separate from intelligence, and which consists of several sub-components – associative memory, inductive language learning ability, grammatical sensitivity, and phonemic coding ability (see Chapter 3). Finally, motivation is seen as the individual's need to study the language in question and his willingness to persevere and overcome obstacles.

In a sense, therefore, Carroll's model is only a subset of the Naiman model, in that it includes some instructional and learner variables, but leaves out others, and it leaves out altogether the context of learning, the process of learning, and learning strategies. Even so, it is of interest because it attempts to be more than a static listing of influences. What Carroll attempts to do is to specify the nature of the interaction between the variables, and to indicate how differences in one variable will constrain the operation of the others. For example, consider the operation of aptitude under conditions of time pressure and moderate instructional quality. Carroll suggests that under these circumstances aptitude will predict fairly well, i.e. it is reasonable to expect an appreciable aptitude–outcome relationship since high-aptitude students will use their abilities to cope with the less-than-perfect instruction and the shortage of time. In contrast, when there is ample time for learning and high-quality instruction, Carroll suggests that aptitude will be a much less potent predictor of language learning success. This is because low-aptitude students can put in more time for learning, and because the quality of instruction, the 'delivery system', will ensure that less-gifted learners are provided with appropriate quantity and quality of instruction. Other combinations of variable conditions can also be examined. Carroll, in fact, provided mathematical functions relating pairs of variables while various assumptions were made about the others. In this way the model attempts to specify the interdependence of different influences on language learning, and goes beyond the taxonomic, 'separate causation' approach shown in Figure 1.2. Although models such as this are very ambitious, they do hold out the hope that ID research and experimental/universalist research can be combined, and the one used to illuminate the other. The Carroll model is discussed here simply because it shows what similar, but more comprehensive and ambitious models could be like. One would like to see more of them developed.

The disjunctive model:
For the sake of completeness, we also need to consider another type of model. This will be termed here the Disjunctive Model, since its main feature is that it accepts that end-states or outcomes can be achieved in different ways. It contrasts with the models which have been described so far. These have all assumed that where there is a correlation between two variables, the relationship between them is linear. In other words, although the strength of the relationship may vary in the different cases, we assume that increases in one variable are matched by increases on the other. When we extend this basic approach to situations where there are several variables, it is assumed that the causal or independent variables can be combined in some sort of simple additive fashion. It is, however, possible that particular outcomes may be achievable by

different routes, and that the different routes may be dependent on different *configurations* of abilities. Focusing on cognitive abilities as an example, it could be that one learner might achieve success via talent for auditory processing of information; another might rely on well-developed visual memory abilities. The end-point they achieve would be similar, but the means they employ to reach that state could be very different.

There are hardly any developed models of this sort in the second language acquisition field. However, there is research, both in first and second language acquisition, which is consistent with such a position (Nelson 1981; Skehan 1986b). It is likely, in fact, that this class of model will become more common in the future, as the diversity of language learners is more fully appreciated, and as interaction effects are properly understood. Spolsky's work (forthcoming) on the use of an expert systems approach to analysing second language learning data is promising in this regard, as are the use of techniques such as cluster analysis (see Chapter 2).

However, these are prospects for the future, not present realities. For present discussion, the chapters that follow will rely primarily on the GLL model to provide an organizing framework, and will consider the potentially more sophisticated interactional and disjunctive models only where these are appropriate. The goal, for the moment, will be the identification of the variables which influence language learning success, and the quantification of these influences. More complex models will be a practical possibility only when these basic relationships have been described adequately.

The plan of the book

Given the preceding discussion on the types of model which may underlie ID research, the rest of this chapter will briefly outline the structure of the book as a whole. Chapter 2 is concerned with methodological issues. It discusses the research techniques which are fundamental for ID research, and also examines some of the less commonly employed alternatives. The following three chapters then take aspects of the model outlined in Figure 1.2, and attempt to survey the relevant research. Chapter 3 focuses on language aptitude. It is proposed that, of all the IDs, foreign language aptitude still generates the most consistent correlations with language learning success. It is argued that aptitude, even though perhaps an unfashionable concept, is not restricted in its operation simply to formal, 'learning' environments, but influences acquisitional processes as well, and can still be the basis for useful theorizing and research. Chapter 4 is concerned with affective influences on language learning. It surveys the research on attitudes and motivation, and the models that have been proposed in this area. It examines the operation of motivational forces in different learning circumstances, and also considers the methodological issues in trying to assess such a complex area. Chapter 5 is concerned with the role of learner strategies. Since the 1970s, research into consciously controllable learner strategies has grown considerably, offering as it does the prospect that we can teach learners how to learn. However, this area has been characterized by conflicting results and also conflicting research techniques. The chapter will examine these different approaches, and assess both the robustness and significance of the findings as well as the effectiveness of the methodologies employed.

Chapters 3, 4, and 5 will, then, examine findings and techniques in three clearly defined areas of ID research. Chapter 6, in contrast, will look at a range of ID variables which are diverse, both in terms of the major areas already mentioned, and in terms of one another. Some cognitive influences on language learning such as intelligence and cognitive style will be covered, and then research into miscellaneous personality variables such as extroversion, sociability, risk-taking, etc. will be discussed.

Chapter 7, in an ideal world, would draw upon a considerable quantity of completed research in examining the nature of the interactions between individual difference variables and the circumstances of learning. It would allow us to bring together the comprehensiveness of a model such as that shown in Figure 1.2 with the dynamic and explanatory power of Carroll's Model of School Learning to account for optimal learning by different individuals in different contexts. It would also provide a framework for the more disjunctive possibilities covered in the fourth model discussed. Unfortunately, aptitude-treatment research of this sort is not extensive. We will be forced to consider a fairly incomplete picture and cover such research as is available while pointing out areas urgently in need of further investigation. There are numerous possibilities here, but little indication that many of them are being exploited currently.

The final chapter examines the role of ID research in second langauge acquisition as a whole. It will be argued that the findings that do exist in ID research have been neglected in mainstream SLA research for too long, and that they should be brought back into greater prominence. They certainly come within the concatenated, or research-then-theory tradition, but it will be argued that the findings that exist need to be an important element for future hierarchical, or theory-then-research approaches. Above all, they will enable us to glimpse the scale of the problem that future hierarchical theories will need to address. Consequently, the concluding discussion is of the strengths and weaknesses of the different approaches to model building in second language learning research.

2

Methodological considerations in ID research

In Chapter 1, the contrast between hierarchical and concatenated approaches to theory construction was covered. It was concluded that even though the hierarchical approach has considerable strengths, the concatenated approach is more appropriate for ID research because of the need to try and quantify the influence of many of the variables that may influence language learning success. In general, ID research, reflecting this research-then-theory orientation, relies on statistical techniques which may not be that familiar to applied linguists and ESOL researchers. Consequently, the present chapter will attempt to provide a brief introduction to the field. More extensive treatment can be found in Hatch and Farhady (1983) and Woods, Fletcher and Hughes (1986). The chapter will first consider issues in questionnaire design and scale construction, and then examine the use of correlational analysis and multivariate statistics. The chapter describes the statistical techniques which underlie the research reported in later chapters. It is, in places, difficult, and so it may be preferable to use the chapter for reference purposes, rather than read through it sequentially.

Questionnaire design and scale construction

Many areas require the use of questionnaires and the construction of self-report scales to assess hypothesized traits. Typical examples in second language learning would be research into attitudes, motivation, learner strategies and personality.

In a sense, each scale of this sort represents a hypothesis on the part of the investigator about an unobservable construct, an hypothesis which has to survive an operationalization into actual test items (by the researcher). The major problem is that the translation from hypothesis to measurement technique is by no means easy, so that such scales are extremely fallible in what they measure, and how well they measure it. The first requirement, therefore, is for the investigator to formulate his hypothesis sufficiently clearly and precisely to enable the generation of items for the scale. The researcher has to specify what the construct is; what the construct is not; and how the construct maps onto actual behaviour. To clarify this rather abstract discussion, we could take the example of anxiety. Mere specification of the 'lay' term anxiety is insufficient. For the concept to be useful much greater precision is needed. Some account has to be given of the functioning and perhaps origin of anxiety. There needs to be clarification as to whether there are dimensions of anxiety. We must be clear whether anxiety is a general-state phenomenon or whether it is situation-specific. We also need to know how anxiety relates to other personality traits. Only if we are clear on all these issues can we begin to devise items and have any hope that they will be successful, doing the job they were intended to.

Once the investigator has clarified whatever construct is meant to underlie a scale, and has generated promising-looking items, there are still two standard pitfalls that need to be guarded against. The first of these is response bias. Some individuals tend to answer positively more often than negatively. If a scale of items is worded so that a positive response always or usually indicates a 'high' score, there is a possibility that some people will obtain such a high score partly because of their response bias. It is important (and fairly simple) to word items so that a high score would be composed of some positive and some negative answers. The second problem concerns social desirability. If answers to particular items can be construed by respondents as 'the desirable answer', then some people will provide this response *even if it is not true*. The item writer has to try and minimize this social desirability influence. Possibly the best approach is to enlist the help of someone else to detect social desirability factors hidden from the writer. This should reduce the 'obviousness' of the desirable answer (although this sometimes results in a certain blandness in the surviving items).

From the above discussion, it is easy to see that *a priori* analysis is insufficient for questionnaire items. There have to be other methods to maximize the chances that effective measurement is achieved. The first such method is to make as many attempts to measure an attitude or trait as possible. Given the fallibility of any *one item*, the best strategy is to generate several, all aimed at the same basic trait, but drawing upon slightly different aspects of it. Different classroom anxiety items might refer to aspects of the teacher's behaviour, other pupils' behaviour, impending examinations, etc. In this way, no individual item carries an excessive load, and an inconsistent response to one item would cause limited damage. But the existence of several items, all of which are meant to be working together, implies that the internal consistency of these items must be investigated empirically. If items are indeed measuring the same basic trait, then they should have positive inter-*item* correlations, i.e. people who answer one item in a particular direction should tend to answer other items similarly. One would expect inter-item correlations in excess of 0.30; items in a scale which do not achieve this level would need to be rejected or rewritten. Alternatively one could examine item-*total* correlations. On the assumption that the total scale measures the trait in question more effectively than single items, a high item-total correlation will indicate that the item in question is contributing to the functioning of the scale as a whole, i.e. is pulling its weight, while low or negative correlations will identify weak items. By means of a cycle of scale administration, item analysis, item acceptance, rejection, or modification, the homogeneity of the scale can be considerably improved, and its reliability increased. One should certainly aim at scales with reliability coefficients in excess of 0.70, and it is preferable to aim for values above 0.80 and 0.90. It is very important that this procedure of scale refinement is followed and that investigators do not use untried, unpiloted scales in actual research studies. If they do, and find no interesting relationships with other variables, they may conclude that no relationships actually exist when in fact all they have shown is that unreliable scales have failed to deliver interesting results. Another fundamental issue to consider is scale validity, i.e. that the scale is measuring what it is intended to measure. Validity is investigated by using the scale in conjunction with other established measures and scales to discover (a) what other measures it correlates with, and (b) what measures it does not correlate with. In the past, scales have often been validated more by only the former of these procedures, i.e. *convergent validity* has been established. Now it is recognized that scales must be shown to be distinct from other scales which purportedly measure other constructs, i.e. *discriminant validity* must be established. It is easier to demonstrate convergent validity than discriminant (Clifford 1981). Two questionnaire-based scales might, for example, inter-relate because of response bias factors. It would look, in this case, as if convergent validity for the trait in question had been established when in fact the relationship would only be reflecting what is essentially error of measurement. Hence the need to establish *both* types of validity, and the need to use multi-trait, multi-method designs (Clifford 1981). And once again, as with reliability, researchers should establish the validity of the scales they use *before* using them in research studies where their worth will be assumed.

Bivariate relationships

Whatever measures are used in ID research, whether they are scales, or performance on tests of some sort, it is of fundamental importance to investigate the relationship between the measures. The present section will focus on relationships between two variables, and in particular, the correlation coefficient technique. The next section will then consider cases where more than two measures are involved, and where multivariate statistical techniques are appropriate.

Interpreting correlation coefficients:
With something like the Good Language Learner Model (Figure 1.2), and an ID research framework, the main tool available to researchers is the correlation coefficient. This index of the association between two variables ranges from a value of + 1, representing a perfect relationship, through 0, suggesting no relationship at all, to − 1, which indicates a perfect negative relationship. In practice, second language learning studies yield correlations whose maximum values rarely approach + 1, and are more likely to be of the order of 0.30 to 0.60. To anticipate some of the findings from future chapters, aptitude and motivation measures (Chapters 3 and 4) often correlate with achievement scores at around these levels. Other influences on language learning success, such as intelligence and field independence (Chapter 6), are more likely to produce correlations at around the 0.30 level. Negative correlations are also possible, and reflect inverse relationships between variables. For example, higher aptitude correlates negatively with the *length of time* needed to reach a certain level of proficiency, i.e. the higher the aptitude, the *less* time it takes to reach a certain level of performance.

Since correlation coefficients are so basic this section will discuss some additional aspects of their use. The first of these is whether a correlation is *significant*. When statistical significance is attained, this means that the results obtained are unlikely to have arisen by chance. For example, if we found a correlation of 0.35 between a measure of risk-taking and a measure of language proficiency, we would first need to establish whether this result is simply the result of chance pairings of high risk-taking and high proficiency scores. In practice, for correlation coefficients, establishing significance is dependent on two factors – the magnitude of the relationship found, and the sample size: the larger the sample size, the lower the correlation required to claim significance. Consequently, it is sensible to use sample sizes which are as large as possible to maximize the chances of attaining significance. Tables are readily available (e.g. Allen and Davies 1977, p. 24) of the correlation values required for significance at different sample sizes.

If significance is achieved, we need to consider the *strength* of the relationship between the variables. We have seen that, in practice, correlations between 0.30 (the lower band for practical interest), and 0.60/0.70 (the highest correlation one is likely to encounter given the multi-causal nature of language learning) are typical. So the frame of reference we have for the interpretation of correlations ranges through 0.30 (weak correlations); 0.40–0.50 (moderate correlation); to 0.60 + (strong correlation). As with some of the other techniques discussed below, an understanding of the meaning of correlation coefficients is really only achieved as one's experience accumulates, and one develops a frame of reference and a set of expectations about what values one is likely to encounter. In addition, it is important to supplement the correlation coefficient itself (a mathematically compressed single index of association) with a visual representation of the relationship between two variables. This visual representation, a *scattergram*, often allows the nature of the relationship to become clearer, e.g. by revealing a couple of outlying values, or perhaps a slightly non-linear relationship.

It is also common practice to square the value of the correlation coefficient, since the result which is obtained represents the proportion of the variation in the scores on one variable which is accounted for by the other. For example, a correlation of 0.60 between (say) aptitude and intelligence, would when squared, give a value of 0.36. This would mean that 36 per cent of the variation in the aptitude scores is accounted for, or is predictable from, the intelligence scores (or vice versa). The square of the correlations coefficient is generally used when more precise indications of the degree of overlap between two variables is required. It should be noted that quite high correlations are needed to account for substantial proportions of the variation in scores on the other variable. The correlation of 0.60 accounts for 36 per cent of the variation – well under 50 per cent. A correlation of 0.70 accounts for 49 per cent of the variation; 0.80 accounts for 64 per cent, and 0.90 for 81 per cent. These figures show (a) that the correlations which are typical in language learning studies do not account for very high proportions of variation in scores, reflecting the multi-causal nature of language learning success, and (b) there are dramatic gains in the proportions of the variation accounted for as one starts to obtain very high correlations, cf. the difference between a correlation of 0.70 and 0.80.

Two further points need to be made about correlations, both of which connect with significance levels. First of all, one should always remember that achieving significance is a function of the strength of the relationship concerned (the really important issue), but also the sample size. This means that it is possible, through the use of a large sample, to achieve significance with a very weak correlation. The establishment of significance is a vital issue, but significance in itself does not mean that the relationship is of great importance – a correlation may be significant but trivial because of its low value. Second, there is the possibility of making mistakes. Significance means that it is unlikely that the correlation could have arisen by chance. This 'unlikeliness' is usually portrayed in terms such as $p < .05$, i.e. that such a result could only have arisen by chance in five studies out of a hundred. What one is doing, therefore, is calculating the improbability of the result having arisen by chance. But improbability is not certainty. The correlation in question *might* have arisen by a freak combination of factors, i.e. there might be no underlying relationship but the chance result might mislead one into thinking that there is. Correspondingly, chance factors might depress a correlation coefficient below the level required for significance even though a real relationship is involved. So establishing significance is a guide, a method of minimizing wrong decisions, but without the guarantee of certainty and absolute truth.

Factors influencing correlations:
Correlations are maximized when each of the variables being correlated is normally distributed, with a good dispersion of scores. This allows maximum opportunity for variation in one measure to be associated with variation on the other. If one (or both) of the variables is restricted in range, e.g. scores are unusually bunched, then the correlations obtained will be lower than if both variables had been normally distributed. An inspection of the dispersion for each variable (e.g. standard deviation, histogram) on a routine basis is sufficient to reveal this danger.

A similar issue is that of reliability. The reliability (or consistency) of measurement is an indication of how much error has crept into test scores. As indicated in the section on questionnaire construction, if there is a lot of error in the scores on a particular measure, reliability will be low. Consequently, the correlations which that measure enters into will be lowered because error, by definition random, is unlikely to correlate with the reliable component of the other variables in the correlation. In other words, low reliability and high error lead to correlations which can be distinctly lower than they might be. Frequently, in fact, when examining a group of correlations, the values involved are largely a function of reliability of measurement, and not of the true relationships involved. (See Henning 1987 for further discussion of this point.)

Attributing causation:
Finally, we have to consider the role of causation. In itself, a correlation coefficient simply reflects the degree of association between two variables, capturing the extent to which high scores on one are matched by high scores on the other. The investigator may well think that one variable is influencing the other, but this conclusion can only be an inference. The correlation coefficient itself is neutral; the inference is in the mind of the researcher, and has to be justified on other, probably theoretical grounds. The problem, basically, is that if two variables, X and Y, are indeed correlated, the association may be the result of one of several factors. X may indeed cause Y. Alternatively, Y may cause X.

There may also be mediation: X may cause Z, which in turn causes Y. Most problematically of all, both X and Y may be caused by Z. An example here might concern the relationship between motivation and language learning success, discussed more extensively in Chapter 4. Suppose an investigator runs a study and establishes a correlation of 0.60 between a measure of motivation and a measure of foreign language learning success. How are we to account for such a result? Most simply, we could say that motivation is the causative variable, with greater levels of motivation leading to greater language learning success. Alternatively, it could be argued that greater success in foreign language learning study engenders positive attitudes, and higher motivation, reversing the direction of causation. But yet another alternative is that language aptitude causes *both* motivation and success. It may cause motivation because greater aptitude makes the language classroom a more interesting place. It may cause success because those with greater aptitude for foreign language study will achieve more highly. The correlation coefficient that we started with is not, in itself, going to provide any basis for choosing amongst those alternatives. For that, appeal to theory or to other research is necessary.

Multivariate statistics

Correlation coefficients provide an index of the association between just two variables. Frequently in language learning research we need to consider sets of more than two variables. In such cases it soon becomes impossible to look at these variables two at a time and make any sense of the *patterns* of results. Larger-scale techniques have to be used to assist human limitations in examining extensive datasets, and so multivariate statistical techniques have been developed.

Factor analysis:
Logically, the first multivariate technique we need to consider is factor analysis, since this technique attempts to uncover the underlying structure of a set of measures. We will start with a clarifying example from the field of language testing. Milanovic (1988) wanted to develop a test battery to measure the language achievement of a group of students receiving English instruction in Hong Kong. He posited that he needed tests in the areas of listening; grammar; appropriacy (i.e. the ability to say something that is not merely correct, but also appropriate to the situation at hand); and reading and writing. Accordingly he devised several sub-tests of each of these four skill areas. However, to establish that his hypothesis about the distinctness of these four areas was justified, and that the tests in one area actually measured that area, he needed to establish empirically that the tests in each domain clustered

Table 2.1: Factor analysis of language test battery

Test	Factor 1	Factor 2	Factor 3	Factor 4
Listening 4	.75			
Listening 1	.70			
Listening 5	.65			
Listening 2	.65			
Listening 6	.63			
Listening 3	.62			
Grammar 1		.75		
Grammar 4		.70		
Grammar 2		.63		
Grammar 3		.51		
Appropriacy 1		.38		
Writing 1			.86	
Reading 2			.66	
Writing 2			.60	
Reading 3		.41	.52	
Reading 1			.44	
Appropriacy 2				.75
Appropriacy 3		.41		.55

together, e.g. that performance on all the listening tests was consistent within this area, but was (somewhat) different from that in grammar, appropriacy, etc. Consequently, he subjected the raw data to a factor analysis, obtaining the results shown in Table 2.1.

Factor analysis examines the raw data and tries to find underlying groupings which seem to unite sets of the measures that are being used. These groupings are the factors, and the analysis portrays the influence of each of these underlying factors on actual tests by means of loadings. Such loadings reflect how important the underlying factor is for each test, with loadings varying from -1 through 0 to $+1$. Higher loadings indicate that the test in question is especially well accounted for by the factor in question. For clarity in the table, factor loadings below 0.35 have not been shown – they are too low to be important, and would simply clutter up the table unhelpfully. Further, within each factor, the order of the tests is determined by the size of the loading, so Listening 4 appears first because it had the highest loading on the first factor. This helps to define the factor more clearly. The table shows that four factors seem to underlie the data, i.e. that although there are 18 tests involved in total, they group into four categories, with there being a fair amount of duplication within each category. The six listening tests all load highly on the first factor, i.e. this first factor is deeply implicated in people's performance on each of these listening tests. Similarly, the

Reading and Writing tests all load highly on Factor 3, while two of the three Appropriacy tests load highly on Factor 4. The second factor is the only one with any complications. It does have loadings on all the Grammar tests, but in addition there is a fairly low loading on the first of the Appropriacy tests. So we can infer that what causes the first group of tests to load together is their common dependence on a posited listening skill, that the second group of tests can be inferred to have in common some competence with grammar, etc., etc. And this is the general sequence in the use of factor analysis. The investigator can, by analysing the tests themselves, and then by looking at the factor analysis tables to see which tests group together, explore how good his predictions and explanations of the data really are.

These results, though, are unusually clear (which is why they were chosen for this example). The only slight problems are the 'misplaced' Appropriacy 1 test, and the double loadings of Reading 3 and Appropriacy 3. Here, despite the initial analysis of the tests, the empirical data suggests that each of these tests relies more heavily on a grammatical competence factor than the researcher had originally supposed (and indeed, re-examination of the actual tests in the light of these results revealed evidence of this). Generally, though, predictions were confirmed to a remarkable degree.

Having worked through the example, we now need information on the details of the technique. Factor analysis works originally from a matrix of scores of N individuals on M variables (where 'N' and 'M' represent 'a certain number', e.g. 50 individuals with scores on eight tests). First, a correlation matrix is calculated between all the combinations of variables taken two at a time. Then the factor-analytic procedure *condenses* the data, and attempts to describe the original measurements with as few factors as possible. There are mathematical criteria within factor analysis for deciding when to stop the procedure, i.e. when continuing the process and positing further factors is becoming unrewarding because the new factors do not seem 'underlying' enough (see Henning 1987 for discussion of this point). This stage of factor analysis is determinate, and should produce the same answer time after time (although there are lively and somewhat exaggerated debates on the merits of different methods of factor analysis). However, at this first, data-condensation stage, explanatory power is sacrificed for mathematics. The first factor matrix produced usually (and artificially) concludes that *one* underlying factor, the first factor extracted from the correlation matrix, is of overriding importance, and all the tests or variables seem heavily dependent on it. For that reason it is customary, once data condensation is accomplished, to aim at a second stage, in which the data which has been condensed is redistributed, and shared out between the factors in a way which lends itself to easier psychological interpretation. This is accomplished by a process known as rotation of factors. It produces tables such as that shown as Table 2.1 where, with luck, the characteristics of the tests underlying the various factors admit of clear interpretation of the factor itself.

We can now restate some of the issues involved in factor analysis. The basic procedure consists of three stages: decisions on which tests to include; the actual procedure of factor analysis; and the interpretation of the factor loadings which are generated. While the middle stage is both objective and mathematically determinate, the first and third stages contain very large subjective components. What is included, and what is *not* included in the analysis will have an immense impact on the likely results. Similarly, how the results are interpreted will also need careful scrutiny; so much so, in fact, that it is strongly advised that the technique is best learned on an apprentice basis by doing it with an experienced factor analyst who is used to handling data in this way. (See the chapters by Carroll, Vollmer and Sang, and Farhady in Oller 1983 for illuminating discussion of these points.)

This brings us to the role of theory in factor analysis. It is useful to think of the degree of theorizing in terms of a cline. At one end of the cline would be a sort of trawling operation, based on the inclusion of a large number of measures each separately and fairly weakly justified. This is a level of investigation even prior to the development of con-catenated theory (see Chapter 1). At the other extreme may be clearly worked out theories which make precise predictions as to the rela-tionships that will be found, and the general structure of the factor matrix. This would be a hierarchical or theory-then-research approach. The extremes are presented here in the form of a cline because it is felt that in reality investigators using factor analytic techniques come some-where in the middle. Factor analytic investigations do often have a trawling component, but it is unlikely that the trawling will be entirely open-ended, and it is quite possible that on occasions the predictions that are made about factor structure will be fairly precise. The example which was used is a case in point. There are both 'trawling' and 'precise prediction' aspects of this study, although probably more of the latter. Most strikingly of all in the example though was the clarity of the results, and the degree of match between original theory and actual results, leading to a much more straightforward interpretation than often occurs.

In fact, speaking in terms of a cline makes it clear how wrong it is to think of factor analysis as simply one technique. There are a range of procedures involved, although it is not necessary to go into detail here on this point. (The reader is referred to Kim and Mueller 1978, and Gorsuch 1974 for more extended discussion.) However, it is important to mention one further important distinction, that between exploratory factor analysis and confirmatory factor analysis. The first type of analysis is of the trawling variety: measures are included because they loosely cover a particular area, but with no clear idea as to what the factor structure might be. Standard procedures are then applied, as described above, followed by psychological interpretation. In contrast *confirmatory factor analysis* has much clearer connections with theory. Such a form of analysis is appropriate when theory is sufficiently well worked out and clear in its predictions to specify a model which can be tested for goodness-of-fit against the data. Unsatisfactory results could then lead to the abandonment or at least modification of the model.

The computer programs for confirmatory factor analysis have only become available relatively recently (Joreskog and Sorbum 1981) and so far they have not been used extensively in applied linguistics, although they have had some impact in language testing. It is likely that they will be applied more widely in ID research in coming years. If so, they will reflect, no doubt, a greater accumulation of reliable empirical generalizations, and a consequent move towards more hierarchical theories.

Regression analysis:
In contrast to the explanatory and structural aims of factor analysis, regression analysis is more concerned with achieving prediction. Fundamental to this is a division of variables into independent and dependent groups. Independent variables are those which are assumed to have a causative effect, and act as predict*ors*. Dependent variables are those assumed to be caused, and hence are predict*ed*. The purpose of regression analysis is to combine several independent variables so they jointly achieve a higher level of prediction than any one of them would taken singly.

We can illustrate this technique by discussing some results from a longitudinal study of language learning capacity (see Chapter 3 for more details). The study collected longitudinal data on the same children at three points in time: indices of first language development (2–6 years of age); measures of foreign language aptitude (13 years); and measures of foreign language achievement (14 years). The study was trying to discover whether first language development, on the one hand, and foreign language aptitude, on the other, predict foreign language achievement. Specifically, we consider the problem of predicting French reading ability at age 14 (here, the variable READING) on the basis of two 'aptitude' measures (IQ and inductive language learning ability; INDUCLANG) and two measures of first language development (syntax development at 42 months (MLU42), and vocabulary at 66 months (VOCAB66)). The general correlation matrix is shown in Table 2.2.

The matrix shows that the dependent variable (READING) has high correlations with three of the four independent variables (VOCAB66 – 0.58: IQ – 0.60: and INDUCLANG – 0.63). The task is to know how to combine each of these independent variables to predict most effec-

Table 2.2: Inter-correlations of measures used in regression study

	MLUS42	VOCAB66	I.Q.	INDUCLANG	READING
MLUS42	—	.04	.25	.36	.17
VOCAB66		—	.24	.34	.58
IQ			—	.75	.60
INDUCLANG				—	.63
READING					—

tively. This is achieved by developing a combination formula so that the scores on each variable can be weighted most efficiently. The formula consists of an equation which multiplies each of the scores on the independent variable by an appropriate weight. The general form of the equation, for four independent variables, is y (the dependent variable) $= aX_1 + bX_2 + cX_3 + dX_4 + e$ (where X1 to X4 are the independent variables and 'e' is a constant value). Then the predicted scores ('y' from the formula) can be correlated with the actual scores to see how effective the prediction has been. This special form of the correlation is known as the multiple correlation coefficient.

It might be thought that the multiple correlation in the present case would be very high, given the first-order correlations. It is not, and this result is typical of all regression equations. In fact the multiple correlation achieved is only 0.74. INDUCLANG enters the equation first because it has the highest first-order correlation) and VOCAB66 enters second, since it produces the highest correlation *after the influence of INDUCLANG has been removed*). The actual formula used here is: y = (0.50 × INDUCLANG) + (0.55 × VOCAB66) − 9.54. For example, someone with scores of 37 on the INDUCLANG and 51 on the VOCAB66 tests would be predicted to score (.50 × 37) + (.55 × 51) − 9.54, i.e. 37.01. (The actual score obtained in this particular case was 33, indicating an error of prediction of 4.) No more independent variables enter the equation, i.e. even though there are four independent variables only two of them enter the equation and contribute to prediction. This is because the independent variables inter-correlate. As a result, the joint correlation or prediction from more than one independent variable has to be purged of an overlap component, to establish what amount of prediction is achieved independently and additionally by each new variable. That is why IQ, although it has a higher first-order correlation with the READING score, does not enter the regression equation either before VOCAB66, or indeed after it. The IQ by INDUCLANG correlation of 0.75 means that it does not do enough *additionally to INDUCLANG* to justify inclusion. As a result, the ultimate multiple correlation is higher than any of the first-order correlations, but not massively so.

In general, then, ordinary regression techniques aim more at effective and practical prediction than explanation and understanding, which is something of a limitation (see the discussion in Gardner 1985, Ch. 4). Consequently, increasing attention is currently being paid to more advanced versions of regression which explore complex *patterns* of causation. Causal modelling, or path analysis, is being used increasingly in general psychological research, and now in ID research in language learning. As implemented in computer packages as LISREL (*LI*near *S*tructural *REL*ations) the technique allows the investigator to specify chains of causality which can then be evaluated for goodness of fit against data. The technique is comparable to confirmatory factor analysis in that it allows (indeed it forces) the investigator to specify a model of some precision which is then tested. It is even possible to specify more than one model, with the several models then being evaluated comparatively to see which accounts for the data best. Path analysis (and LISREL in particular) is discussed in Pedhazur (1982), and Long (1983a, 1983b) although these treatments are difficult. An example of the use of LISREL can be found in Gardner (1985, Ch. 8). As we move, in the future, towards a theory-then-research orientation, researchers will want to specify models and test them out. These more advanced statistical techniques will be unavoidable at that point, and are certain to become increasingly common.

Cluster analysis:
In the preceding discussion, the different analytic techniques have assumed two things. First, they take for granted a monotonic or linear relationship between any two variables, i.e. the greater the X, the greater the Y. Second, they assume that different variables are additive in their effects. The first assumption runs into difficulties with non-linear relationships, such as a threshold effect, where to perform adequately on Variable Y, one might need a certain minimum level on Variable X, but no more, and additional capacity would not be an advantage. Phonological discrimination could be an example of this. The second assumption causes problems when we examine *patterns* of relationships. For example, in regression the dependent variable is accounted for by the most effective weighting of the contribution by *all the variables*. But there is the possibility that there may be sub-groups of subjects and that the sets of relationships between variables found in Sub-group A might be different from the sets of relationships found in Sub-group B. Analysing a data matrix as if everyone is the same might obscure the relationships that would emerge clearly if the groups were analysed separately and *patterns* of independent variables shown to have special importance, e.g. where learners can achieve success by either auditory or visual learning (Reid 1986). A composite regression equation might distort differences between the two groups because it

aims at developing one equation. What would be more important would be to establish, at the outset, what sub-groups of students might exist, and then develop separate regression equations for each.

Essentially, the purpose of cluster analysis is to identify sub-groups of subjects who are maximally similar to one another, and different from other sub-groups of subjects. So the end-point of cluster analysis is not a reduced number of variables, but a reduced number of subjects, or *subject types*. There are three major steps in cluster analysis. The first is the calculation of a similarity or dissimilarity matrix. At this stage, each subject is compared (on the basis of scores on all variables) with all the other subjects. For each comparison an index is calculated. Given the starting matrix, cluster analysis then enters a second stage of agglomeration. The similarity matrix is scanned for the two subjects whose pattern of scores relates most highly (or for dissimilarity measures, whose scores differ the least). These two subjects are then fused, and a composite score on the variables is calculated to represent the first 'supersubject'. The matrix of subjects has therefore been reduced by one. Next, a new similarity (or dissimilarity) matrix is calculated, incorporating the 'supersubject' and all the remaining subjects, and the next agglomeration cycle takes place. The process can then continue until all the subjects have been agglomerated into one cluster. This brings us to the final stage of cluster analysis – the decision as to when to stop clustering. Cluster analysis provides no automatic decision criteria for this, simply information which can be the basis for an investigator's judgement – a judgement which is therefore somewhat subjective. This judgement, though, is constrained by two types of evidence. Cluster analysis provides a mathematical index of the 'looseness' in the clusters at each stage of the agglomerative procedure. This measure, known as the error sum of squares, frequently shows sudden jumps, reflecting much greater looseness as new clusters are formed at certain stages of the analysis. The investigator may regard these points, or rather the number of clusters prior to the introduction of sudden looseness, to be worth investigating, and may suspend the clustering at such points to examine whether the clusters formed have some psychological interpretability. An alternative procedure is to use a visual representation of the closeness of the different clusters, known as a dendogram, which represents diagrammatically the distance between the clusters which are being fused. Where excessive distance is involved in a new cluster fusion the investigator may feel that the natural structure and grouping in the data is being violated, and stop clustering just prior to that point. (See Skehan 1986b for a cluster analysis example, and Woods *et al*. 1986 for general discussion of the technique.)

Cluster analysis is not as developed as factor analysis. Relatively few studies use it, and there is less consensus on its procedures. There has also been a dearth of widely available computer packages. However this situation is changing. CLUSTAN (Wishart 1978) is becoming increasingly common, and SPSSPC now has a cluster analysis procedure (Norusis 1986). It seems likely that the technique will be used much more extensively in the future, as Disjunctive Models and studies of learner types become more common.

3

Language aptitude

This chapter will discuss one of the central individual differences in language learning – that of language aptitude. There are five sections to the chapter. The first examines the 'classical' period of aptitude research, and the development of aptitude test batteries. This is followed by a review of recent research on the origin of aptitude. Then the use of aptitude information to characterize learners' strengths and weaknesses is considered, followed by an extended discussion of some of the critiques that have been levelled against the concept of aptitude. The final section relates aptitude to second language acquisition and models of communicative competence.

The development of aptitude batteries

In the first half of this century various attempts were made, e.g. Henmon *et al* (1929) and Symonds (1930), to devise aptitude test batteries. These early attempts suffered from two major drawbacks. First, the correlations with achievement scores that they generated were not very impressive. Second, they seemed excessively dependent on a grammar–translation methodology. (See Carroll 1965, 1981 for discussion of this work.)

What could be termed the 'modern' view of aptitude originated in the 1950s with the work of Professor J.B. Carroll who, with Stanley Sapon, produced the most well known aptitude battery of all – the Modern Languages Aptitude Test (MLAT: Carroll and Sapon 1957). There is no more instructive way of finding out about language aptitude than following the stages that Carroll and Sapon took in the construction of the MLAT. Given the shortcomings of the then existing batteries, Carroll and Sapon came up with the following set of guidelines for the development of *new* potential aptitude tests.

1 Tests of the ability to mimic sounds and stretches of sounds: (a) the length of the 'mimicry span', (b) the accuracy with which unusual sounds can be imitated.
2 Measures of native-language oral-production speech style.
3 Various dimensions isolated by factor analysis, e.g. a rote-memory factor and various fluency factors.
4 Tests of phonetic discrimination.
5 Work sample tests of language learning.
6 Phonemic accuracy measures under conditions of distraction.
7 Tests of the ability to imitate foreign accents.
8 Tests of flexibility with foreign language orthography.
9 Tests of the ability to develop meanings inductively.

In a more recent review article Carroll (1981) modestly remarks that 'this list of traits was only marginally on target'. At the next stage of the research, Carroll and Sapon devised a large number of tests based on the above criteria, generally including more than one test in each area. (Forty-five tests were involved in all (Carroll 1965)). These tests were given to large numbers of language learners at the beginning of their courses of study; end-of-course achievement scores were also collected; and the two sets of scores were correlated. Carroll and Sapon were then in a position to do two things. First, they were able to reject those predictor tests which did not have significant correlations with the achievement test scores. Second, they could also reject tests which duplicated one another, i.e. tests which intercorrelated highly. To help in the task of eliminating duplication, and identifying the 'underlying' number of aptitude traits, Carroll and Sapon factor-analysed their data. From these analyses, Carroll (1965) put forward what has now become the standard 'four component' view of language aptitude. The components postulated are:

1 Phonemic Coding Ability
2 Grammatical Sensitivity
3 Inductive Language Learning Ability
4 Rote learning activity for foreign language materials

Phonemic Coding Ability: Early in his research, Carroll concluded that the ability to make isolated sound discriminations was of limited relevance for language aptitude. Instead, he focused on a *sound–symbol association ability*, i.e. the ability to make a link between sound and symbol. However, Carroll later renamed this as a phonemic coding ability, with a new emphasis on the capacity to discriminate and *code foreign sounds in such a way that they could be recalled later*. Merely associating sound and symbol is not enough – more important are the ability to impose some sort of analysis on the unfamiliar foreign sounds and also the ability to transform the sound into a form more amenable to storage. Even more recently Carroll (1979) has speculated that what is involved relates to the ability to spell and handle phonetic-ortho-graphic material.

Grammatical Sensitivity: This is the ability to recognize the grammatical functions that words fulfil in sentences. One might think that such an ability (a) may be differentially related to different methods of language teaching, and (b) is susceptible to training and experience (in which case one may be dealing not with any innate ability but simply with relevant past experience). Both these points would suggest that Grammatical Sensitivity is an artifact of the way languages are taught, and so would rule out some people being simply more able to deal with grammatical aspects of language than others. For the first criticism there is little direct evidence. All one can say is that the Words in Sentences sub-test has proved to be the most robust of all the sub-tests used in the language aptitude field, and withstands study-to-study variation. There is more evidence on the issue of trainability. Politzer and Weiss (1969) attempted to 'improve aptitude' through instruction, but found the Words in Sentences sub-test to be only marginally affected. Carroll (1979) suggests that the Words in Sentences sub-test has low correlations with previously reported grammatical instruction but higher correlations with a general reasoning test and self-reports of current grammatical ability. Carroll interprets this as a capacity to profit from instruction in this area: lack of exposure to such instruction may well prove a handicap, but presence of such exposure is no guarantee of success since the ability to exploit this instruction may be lacking.

Inductive Language Learning Ability: Carroll (1973) defines this as 'the ability to examine language material and from this to notice and identify patterns of correspondence and relationships involving either meaning or syntactic form', i.e. to be able to infer from limited evidence – an aspect of general reasoning ability that is particularly important in the language learning domain. This ability is obviously close to the construct of grammatical sensitivity. However, grammatical sensitivity seems more connected with analysing a given language structure, while inductive language learning ability emphasizes reasoning and extrapolating. More research on the distinction between these two factors would be desirable.

Memory and Learning: Following the tenets of associationistic psychology, dominant in the period when the MLAT was developed, Carroll conceived this ability to involve the bonding or 'stamping in' of connections between stimuli (native language words), and responses (target language words). He was proposing, that is, that people vary in the efficiency with which they make such bonds, vary therefore in speed of vocabulary growth, and consequently in FL achievement.

The trialling of many potential predictor tests, the subsequent statistical analyses, and the postulation of underlying constructs were only the starting point for the development of actual aptitude measurement instruments which could, when used by non-researchers, predict language learning in the most efficient and practical way possible. The aim here was to find a set of tests which (a) sample the four factors, and (b) duplicate one another as little as possible. Five sub-tests were eventually chosen to make up the Modern Languages Aptitude Test (MLAT) (Carroll and Sapon 1959). The five sub-tests of the full form are:

Part One: Number Learning: The student is taught, on tape, the Kurdish number system from 1 to 4, plus the 'tens' and 'hundreds' forms of these numbers, then tested by hearing numbers which are combinations of these elements, e.g. 312, 122, 41, etc. The test aims at measuring associative memory. *Part Two: Phonetic Script*: This sub-test measures phonemic coding ability. The student learns a system of phonetic notation for some English phonemes. He is then tested on this learning, e.g. 'Underline the word you hear: Tik; Tiyk; Tis; Tiys'. *Part Three: Spelling Clues*: This is a highly speeded test that measures both native language vocabulary and phonemic coding ability. The student is given clues to the pronunciation of a word, e.g. 'ernst' for 'earnest', and is then asked to choose a synonym from a list of alternatives. *Part Four: Words in Sentences*: This tests grammatical sensitivity. In a typical item, two sentences are presented, with one word in the first sentence underlined. In the second sentence five words are underlined. The student has to decide which of the underlined words in the second sentence fulfils the same function as the underlined word in the first sentence. *Part Five: Paired Associates*: The student studies a written Kurdish–English vocabulary list, practices the stimulus-response pairs seen, and is then tested by means of multiple-choice items. This is a test of associative memory.

In general the total score of the MLAT yields multiple correlations of between 0.40 to 0.60. This can even rise to a figure of 0.70 under favourable prediction conditions, i.e. heterogeneous students and intensive courses (cf. the Carroll Model of School Learning discussed in Chapter 1). The figure is correspondingly reduced if one is dealing with homogeneous (perhaps streamed) students, and/or when the teaching is non-intensive. Overall, these levels of multiple correlation are encouraging, since they are higher than one would obtain from intelligence measures. On the other hand, the figures are well short of unity, implying that there are many other influences on language learning, and that aptitude is not the whole story.

There are several slightly different forms of the MLAT available. The MLAT itself is for use with people of 14 years of age and above. There is also an elementary form (EMLAT) for use with children between the ages of eight and eleven. In addition, there are forms of the

MLAT available for blind students, and for L1s other than English, such as Italian (Ferencich 1964). French (Wells *et al*. 1982), and Japanese (Murakami 1974). There is also a short form of the test, for use when time is limited. So it can be seen that a diverse set of materials, all based on the four-factor model, can be used for the assessment of aptitude.

We have concentrated so far on the work of J.B. Carroll. It should be mentioned, though, that a comparable battery exists – the Pimsleur-Language Aptitude Battery (LAB: Pimsleur 1966, 1968), appropriate for children aged 13 to 19. Compared to the MLAT, the LAB emphasizes inductive language learning capacities and auditory ability. The latter emphasis arises because Pimsleur did research (Pimsleur, Sundland and McIntyre 1966) which suggested that 20 to 30 per cent of children underachieve in foreign language learning because they have poor auditory ability, *even though other components of aptitude are at normal levels*. What the LAB does *not* have, in comparison with the MLAT, is a test of grammatical sensitivity, on the one hand, and any effective coverage of memory, on the other. Pimsleur, that is, seems to regard language aptitude as consisting of a language analytic ability and an auditory ability. Carroll's view is broader. He matches Pimsleur's one inductive language learning ability sub-test with a test of grammatical sensitivity (MLAT4). But the MLAT1 (Number Learning) and MLAT5 (Paired Associates) have no equivalents in the Pimsleur test. One assumes that this is very much a reflection of Carroll's background in psychology and learning while Pimsleur's greater involvement in linguistics focuses more on syntax and sounds.

It is striking now, more than two decades after the MLAT and LAB appeared, how little impact these batteries currently have, either practically or theoretically, and how little additional research has been conducted. Occasional investigators have examined limited aspects of aptitude, and, in many ways, our understanding of aptitude has been deepened as a result. But no-one has really challenged the overall framework established by Carroll and Pimsleur, and reviewed very thoroughly in Carroll (1981). The following section will review the rather piecemeal research conducted since the mid 1960s.

One strand of research (Culhane 1971, Natelson 1975) has been to carry out validation studies of existing batteries. Another has been to develop aptitude batteries for use in particular countries. In Britain, for example, Davies (1971a, b) and Green (1975a, b) have worked along these lines. In each case, the beginnings of an aptitude battery emerged, but not a comprehensive measuring instrument. However, in the case of the York study (Green 1975a), one of the tests developed, the York Language Analysis Test, has been widely used in Britain. Somewhat surprisingly, there has been little research, however, into batteries aimed at specific proficiency skills, e.g. listening, or alternatively into batteries for particular target language types, e.g. tone languages.

The most important research aimed at the production of a new test battery has been carried out by the American Armed Forces. Dissatisfaction had been felt because the MLAT failed to discriminate adequately at higher levels. Accordingly an amalgam of two existing aptitude batteries, Al-Haik's AFLAAT (Al-Haik 1972), and Horne's Language Aptitude Test (Horne 1971, cited in Petersen and Al-Haik 1976) were put together, administered and subjected to considerable statistical investigation. The original set of nine sub-tests was reduced, through factor analysis, to three factors. Two general problems emerged with this research. First of all, the statistical analyses were aimed at maximizing prediction. As a result, the psychological relevance of the factors was sacrificed in the cause of obtaining higher levels of prediction. Second, the increase in prediction that was achieved was marginal. In a comparative study, the multiple correlations reported for the DLAB were of the order of 0.44, and those for the MLAT were also around this level (Petersen and Al-Haik 1976). Subsequent research with another sample which only used the DLAB produced multiple correlations of the order of 0.52 (although since MLAT figures are not provided for this later sample, we do not know whether it, too, might have yielded higher values). In any case, it can be seen that the improvement is only very slight, and also limited to one situation for which the DLAB was finely tuned. One cannot anticipate, therefore, that any fresh insights or applications will be developed from the research.

Another type of aptitude research has been to examine one component of aptitude in greater depth. This basically is what has happened with memory, which, in the MLAT, is conceived as associative memory. In fact, associative memory is only a limited aspect of memory, and so research by Skehan (1980, 1982) has considered several other aspects of its functioning. The first of these is Size of Working Memory. Psychologists now consider the human memory system to have a number of components. Many psychologists have proposed that all incoming information (e.g. language) has to pass through a temporary, limited-capacity working memory (Baddeley and Hitch 1974) before it can enter our permanent store of knowledge (if it ever does!). Greater working memory size might therefore be an advantage in foreign language learning. Response Integration was also investigated in the Skehan (1982) study. The psychologist George Mandler (1967, 1979) has criticized associative memory theories for focusing too much on the association or bond between the stimulus and the response, and has proposed that more effort should be put into studying the nature of the response term itself. Skehan (1982) hypothesized that the need to consider the response term becomes even more important when we are working in a foreign language context. Skehan (1982) also examined Memory for Text, since recently in cognitive psychology much more attention has been paid to memory for meaningful material in general and to connected text in particular. It was hypothesized that an ability to analyse text, to extract its propositional content, and remember such content would be related to greater foreign language learning success.

It was found that working memory size did not relate to language learning success (correlating with achievement at 0.12 only). In retrospect, one can speculate that working memory *size* may be less important than how effectively information is *analysed* and how quickly working memory can be purged (Clark and Clark 1977) during language processing. The two remaining tests – those of response integration and memory for text – produced much more impressive correlations at 0.55 and 0.57 respectively. The first correlation confirms that foreign language learners need to assimilate vast quantities of unfamiliar-sounding material. Small wonder then, that those who are better at doing this experience greater foreign language learning success. Equally, the ability to use previous syntactic, semantic and pragmatic knowledge to analyse incoming language may well be a very basic one which carries over into the learning of foreign languages. What the memory-for-text predictor seems to do is measure how adept people are at bringing their general knowledge of meaning to bear on newly presented material; to see relationships between the elements involved; and to relate them to existing knowledge (Widdowson 1983).

Recent research on the origin of aptitude

Recently some studies have been carried out which probe the origin of language aptitude. The studies have all been based on follow-up research to the Bristol Language Project (Wells 1981, 1985), referred to in Chapter 2, which studied the *first* language development of a representative sample of 129 children born in the Bristol area in the years 1969–70 and 1971–72. The Bristol Project (Wells 1985) reported, amongst other findings, that there are massive individual differences between the children in rate of language development (thus undermining one of Neufeld's (1978) main supporting arguments against the concept of foreign language aptitude: his claim that IDs do not exist in native language learning). Subsequent phases of the Bristol Project have examined the transition to schooling for some of the children and have indicated that schooling, at least up to age 10, seems to consolidate differences that children bring on entry to school, rather than removing them. The follow-up to the Bristol Project was carried out when the children reached secondary school, and started foreign language study. The basic research design is shown in Figure 3.1. The research was therefore examining whether success in foreign language learning is related to speed of first language development; and whether aptitude is,

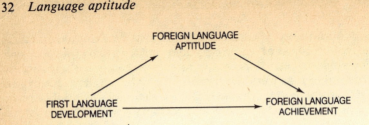

FOREIGN LANGUAGE
APTITUDE

FIRST LANGUAGE
DEVELOPMENT

FOREIGN LANGUAGE
ACHIEVEMENT

Figure 3.1: The research design for the Bristol follow-up research

in any way, a 'residue' (Carroll 1973) of this first language learning capacity.

Basically, the results obtained (covered in much greater detail in Skehan 1986a, 1986c, Skehan 1988, in press a, in press b) give some, but not complete support to the autonomous, pre-programmed language learning capacity viewpoint. There are several correlations above 0.40 between first language measures of developing syntax (e.g. mean morpheme length of utterance, noun phrase complexity) and language aptitude. Since the first language measures were obtained at around three and a half years of age and the aptitude indices at 13 or 14, these results are remarkable. In analyses currently in progress, there are indications that some aspects of first language syntax development such as the growth of the auxiliary system, and the use of pronominalization, correlate particularly well with subsequent aptitude. These syntactic features, labelled 'fragile' by Goldin-Meadow (1982), may provide clues about the central features of an autonomous language processing ability.

However, there are also complicating findings since the correlations between the first language indices and foreign language *achievement* are lower than those between first language and aptitude. Possibly the underlying language learning capacity is the same at different ages, i.e. three and 13, but the learning situation differs. School-based language learning, it could be argued, is an entirely different proposition from child language acquisition and so one would not expect high correlations to emerge between them. Following this line of argument, the correlation between first language acquisition and aptitude reflects the way aptitude measures tap underlying language learning capacities *which are not exploited in language teaching classrooms*.

The above interpretation, however, suggests that aptitude relates more to first language learning ability than to foreign language achievement. In fact, the correlations between aptitude and achievement were amongst the highest of all (Skehan 1988). This paradox was examined through series of regression analyses which were run to try to establish exactly what factors predict the aptitude test scores. The aptitude tests were the dependent variables in these analyses, and the first language measures were the independent variables. In almost all the regression analyses the first variable to enter the equation was measure of social class, vocabulary development, or parental education. In next place came some aspect of first language development which reflected syntactic growth. A typical regression is shown in Table 3.1. In Table 3.1 the respective values are 0.55 (Family Background) and 0.52 (Mean Length of Utterance at 42 months), and taken together they yield a multiple correlation of 0.68, which accounts for 47 per cent of the variance in the aptitude score. (Fuller details are provided in Skehan 1986c and Skehan 1988.)

Table 3.1: Regression on EMLAT2: Matching words

Variable	Multiple R	R^2
Family background	.55	.31
MLUS42 months	.68	.47

The conclusion here seems to be that aptitude scores are predictable from two main sources. The first, and most important, connects social class, vocabulary development, and parental education. The second relates to the pre-programmed autonomous language learning ability we discussed earlier, and can be described as a generalized capacity to process syntax. For purposes of achieving a theoretical understanding of aptitude it is clearly the second influence which is important, and it is disappointing that, significant though this is, the primary influence is clearly elsewhere. We are left, that is, with limited support for the initial hypothesis, since we can propose that aptitude tests do reflect this language processing capacity but that it is not an aspect of aptitude that goes on to connect with foreign language achievement. The implication here is that it is the social class linked group of factors which accounts for the aptitude–achievement set of relationships, a claim which is supported by the finding that the same set of variables – social class, vocabulary development, parental education – enter into significant, and often high (above 0.50), relationships at the first-order level with foreign language achievement.

One explanation of these findings may be through the concept of decontextualized or context-disembedded language (Donaldson 1978). The argument is that the skills and capacities needed to use such language are different from those involved when language is simply an outgrowth of a real, current situation. In the former case, language is a symbolic tool which can be used to look in upon itself. In the latter it is a direct reflection of experience. It has also been argued that the use of decontextualized language is class-linked (Tizard and Hughes 1984), with middle-class parents tending to provide more exposure to such language use. And, crucially, this is the aspect of language functioning that is the greatest prerequisite for successful performance within an educational setting. It is here that children are expected to see the generality of the school experiences and to abstract and go beyond the actual classroom events and information they encounter in their thinking and their writing. This connects with the Bristol Project finding that success at age 10 relates most strongly to the preparedness for literacy of the children on entry to school, with schooling consolidating rather than eliminating the school-entry IDs. What we are seeing in the aptitude-based follow-up research is that these factors continue to exert an influence several years later even in the specific subject of foreign language study.

If we return now to aptitude tests, it is clear that they work because of their hybrid nature. They partly measure an underlying language learning capacity which is similar in first and foreign language learning settings. But their main emphasis is probably in their capacity to function as a measure of the ability to learn from decontextualized material. To do well on an aptitude test, that is, one has to draw on language abilities *and*, more importantly, the ability to cope with decontextualized material. Both of these capacities are important in foreign language achievement, and hence the effective prediction achieved through aptitude tests.

Characterizing strengths and weaknesses

Although one can take aptitude as a monolithic, undifferentiated construct, it is more fruitful, in educational terms, to emphasize the multi-component basis of aptitude, since this provides a framework for the study of learner strengths and weaknesses. So, for example, one might consider the case of someone who scores highly on inductive language learning ability (say), and poorly on phonemic coding ability. More generally, (and collapsing, for the sake of simplicity, into one factor of language analytic ability the two constructs of inductive language learning ability and grammatical sensitivity), if one dichotomizes each variable into high or low one can imagine the possibilities shown in Table 3.2.

Learner types 1 and 8 are straightforward. They represent learners who are strong (1) or weak (8) in all areas. More interesting are the 'mixed' types. Learner 5, for example, has poor phonemic coding ability, but is good otherwise, i.e. at analysis and at assimilating large quantities of material. In contrast, Learner 7 only has a good memory, so that the route to success in this case would have to exploit the area of strength identified.

Table 3.2: Logically possible learner types

	Phonemic coding ability	Language analytic ability	Memory	
1	+	+	+	General, even high aptitude
2	+	+	−	Good auditory and analytic ability, poor memory
3	+	−	+	Good auditory and memory abilities; Poor analysis
4	+	−	−	Good auditory ability; Poor otherwise
5	−	+	+	Poor auditory; Good analysis and memory
6	−	+	−	Poor auditory and memory; Good analysis
7	−	−	+	Poor auditory and analysis Good memory
8	−	−	−	Evenly poor aptitude

This more differentiated view of aptitude could be the basis for more effective teaching, for capitalizing upon strengths and compensating for weaknesses, and also of counselling students based on more accurate information as to their likely accomplishments. Take Learner 5, for example. Here (at least) two courses of action seem possible. One might handle the low phonemic coding ability by offering compensating, auditory-based individualized instruction, or intensive pre-course tuition. More radically, of course, Learner 5 students could be advised to take a reading course, since they might experience frustration with more oral/aural teaching.

The discussion so far has been of logical possibilities. It is striking, though, how little actual research has been done to exploit aptitude information to characterize learner strengths and weaknesses. This is all the more surprising given Pimsleur's original interest in diagnostic aptitude testing (Pimsleur *et al.* 1966) and the more recent attempts to promote individualized instruction (Altman and James 1980, Geddes and Sturtridge 1982). There are, in fact, two lines of research which are easily possible. The first attempts to validate the components of aptitude in diagnostic terms. Such research would take the three-component model of aptitude as a starting framework and try to study the educational consequences of treating different learner types in different ways. The second type of research would attempt to uncover learner types, on an empirical or theoretical basis, using aptitude data but without any preconceptions about the categories involved. One study of each type can be described.

Wesche (1981) reports on the work done by the Public Service Commission of Canada to improve the efficiency of its language instruction. MLAT and LAB sub-test scores, in conjunction with counselling and interview data, were used to assign groups of students to various language teaching methodologies. Three groups of students were involved. First, there was a general group, who had even-shaped profiles on the aptitude sub-tests. These students were assigned to an audiolingual methodology. A second group contained students who had high scores on the Words in Sentences sub-test from the MLAT. These students were taught by an analytic method. Another group of students whose Words in Sentences score was low, but who had compensatingly high memory and phonetic coding abilities were assigned to a 'Situational Approach'. It was found that this basis for group assignment worked well, and produced greater satisfaction and achievement amongst students matched with appropriate methods. The 'interaction' or 'condition-seeking' aspect of this research will be covered more fully in Chapter 7.

The second study to be reported (Skehan 1986b) simply takes a group of learners and tries to identify sub-groups amongst them. Several aptitude sub-test scores were obtained for Army personnel receiving intensive instruction in colloquial Arabic. Measures included verbal intelligence, grammatical sensitivity, analytic memory, associative memory, and response integration. In addition, age was included as a variable, together with criterion test performance (a composite test of spoken colloquial Arabic). These data were subjected to a cluster analysis, in which the attempt was made to establish *learner types* completely empirically. Basically three types of learner were revealed. The first group consisted of a family of clusters, characterized in each case by a flat profile but at different levels. These were learners without particular strengths or weaknesses relative to their general level of performance. More interesting were the other two clusters, each successful on the criterion test scores. One successful group was characterized as young, having good memories, but with grammatical sensitivity only slightly above average. The other was considerably older, fairly average in memory, but much higher in grammatical sensitivity. The first successful group achieved its success through greater reliance on memory, which was probably used to assimilate large amounts of material without much analysis. The other group achieved success through more impressive language-analytic abilities and the capacity to organize and structure material. Possibly because of greater age, there was less impressive memory ability, so the group may have learned to use analytic abilities more effectively to compensate for memory shortcomings.

Two points can now be made about the learner type research. A minor point is simply to note the correspondence between the Wesche and Skehan studies. In each case, three learner types have been proposed – an even-profiled learner; an analytic learner; and a memory-based learner. The major point is to connect this aptitude research with contemporary linguistics. Although most linguists aim at the parsimonious and elegant description of language structure, this view has recently come under some attack. In terms of *acquisition*, Peters (1983) proposes that the units of the linguist need not be, and are not likely to be, the units of the language learner. Learners, she proposes, frequently operate with chunks of language on an 'analyse only if you have to' principle. These chunks could potentially (in linguistic terms) be related to one another and therefore stored and produced more economically, but a language user (or learner) will not necessarily carry out such analyses if (a) the separate chunks function effectively in conveying the meanings intended, and (b) the learner is equipped with a memory system which can tolerate this inefficiency and redundancy. Bolinger (1975) has argued that, more generally, the analysability of language itself is a fiction, or at least an overestimate that is convenient for linguists, and Pawley and Syder (1983) propose that language *performance* is often based on heavily lexicalized sentence stems which draw upon a very large memory bank, rather than on a fully generative linguistic model.

The aptitude research seems to embrace both the linguistic and the 'chunking' viewpoints, however, suggesting two different *orientations* to language development – one linguistic, and one memory-based. One type of learner seems to have a language learning orientation which stresses the analysability of language while the other, perhaps more expression-oriented, is more apt to rely on chunks of language and efficient memory. It is even possible that the different learner types derive from different preferences in information processing arising from hemispherical lateralization: Wesche and Schniederman (nd) have speculated that analytic, sequential styles may implicate the left hemisphere, while holistic and parallel-processing orientations may be associated with the right hemisphere. Carroll (1981) has similarly speculated that MLAT sub-tests may rely differently on the functioning of the two hemispheres. Viewed against this background, the aptitude research which has suggested the existence of learner types is corroborated and strengthened. What the aptitude research may have been reflecting is the existence of two contrasting orientations to language and language learning. One would like to see further research to extend these insights and to develop appropriate teaching materials for learners of these differing orientations.

Critiques of language aptitude: a review

Language aptitude has not been a fashionable concept in the past few years, and has been associated with a number of criticisms. These will now be reviewed, partly to enable them to be evaluated and partly because they provide a framework for the wider discussion of aptitude.

1: Other factors are much more important than aptitude

It has been proposed that motivation (Gardner 1985), or cognitive style (McDonough 1981), or degree of acculturation (Schumann 1978, Neufeld 1978) or personality and attitude (Hubbard 1975) are of greater significance than aptitude. This criticism is really an empirical question, and what is needed is evidence. In fact, such evidence as is available from quantification-based studies generally demonstrates that aptitude is *at least as important*, and usually more important, than any other variable investigated. Studies have reported multiple correlations between aptitude battery totals and criterion scores as high as 0.70, and values of 0.50 are commonplace. Only motivation indices even approach such high figures. The values one obtains for personality measures and traits such as cognitive style are considerably lower, rarely going much above 0.30 (see Chapters 4 and 6).

In fact, what is most striking is that the superiority of variables other than aptitude has often been *assumed*, with the result that a measure of aptitude is often not even included in research studies (see, for example, the dismissal of aptitude in Schumann's work, when an alternative, and unchecked explanation for the failure of learners such as Alberto would simply be that they have low aptitude). The generalization can be offered, therefore, that aptitude is consistently the most successful predictor of language learning success, and failure to include some attempt to measure aptitude will render the interpretation of any research study very difficult.

2: Aptitude is fixed and innate

This, too, is an empirical question in principle, although a much more subtle and fundamental one to answer clearly. Certainly one relevant issue would be to examine the influence of previous learning and experience upon current language learning. Unfortunately most of the evidence in this area is anecdotal, and also usually confounds aptitude with previous learning experiences, i.e. those who have been more successful in the past may have had more aptitude and may also now be more articulate about their current learning experiences, so that it is difficult to disentangle the effects of aptitude from these other factors. Research into the effects of training on aptitude test performance is more clear cut. Politzer and Weiss (1969) attempted to train learners to perform better on the component sub-tests of the MLAT, in general, unsuccessfully. Drawing on these and other studies (e.g. Yemi-Komshian 1965). Carroll (1981, p. 86) reflected:

> I have no hard evidence that would impel me to disagree with the idea that foreign language aptitude, considered as the individual's initial state of readiness and capacity for learning a foreign language, and probable degree of facility in doing so, is crucially dependent upon past learning experiences. Yet, what evidence I have suggests that foreign language aptitude is relatively fixed over long periods of an individual's life span, and relatively hard to modify in any significant way.

It is also important to say that the evidence reported in the follow-up research to the Bristol Language Project (Skehan 1986c; 1988; in press, a, b;) is consistent with this conclusion since it too suggests aptitude stability, i.e. significant correlations with measures taken more than 10 years apart. The implication is that some language learning abilities emerge by the age of three and a half, with the Bristol-linked research not being able to resolve the issue of whether the abilities are innate and/or influenced by the early environment prior to this age.

3: Aptitude is undemocratic and unfair

This value judgement presupposes aptitude is innate and/or stable, that some people have more of it than others, and that those with less can do nothing to alter their capacities. These propositions conflict with two major thrusts of contemporary applied linguistics – the focus on universal processes, on the one hand, and the continuing attempts to identify 'superior' forms of instruction, on the other.

There are several lines of defence against this 'undemocratic' argument. We need to know the capabilities of language learners if we are to design courses effectively. If learners differ in their capacity and speed of learning, as Wesche (1981) indicates, then we need to know about such attributes so that syllabuses and methodologies can reflect them. This might involve gathering the information which could be the basis for streaming, a conventional response to mixed-ability groups. More imaginatively it might lead to the modification of teaching strategies in the direction of cyclical syllabuses, or core plus satellite approaches. Perhaps most interestingly of all, it might involve the tailoring of courses. The area of individualization has grown in importance in recent years, but it is striking to what extent such work merely allows the proliferation of alternative learning paths without the reference to the characteristics of the learner. It is as if simply choice in itself is sufficient, without attention being paid to the principles on which choices need to be based, e.g. aptitude-based learner characteristics.

More generally (and anticipating Chapter 7), the probable existence of learner types means that different types of instruction may be effective with different types of learner. Analytically oriented learners could be provided with analytically oriented materials at appropriate levels. Memory-oriented learners could similarly be provided with suitable material which would suit their predisposition to assimilate unanalysed material. Aptitude information, that is, would be used to maximize the level of proficiency achieved, and increase the *rate* at which different learner types progress. After all, aptitude is defined, following Carroll, in terms of the *rate* of learning, and *not* in terms of some people being incapable of successful foreign language study.

4: Aptitude is relevant to formal teaching situations only

This criticism, in recent years, has been mainly associated with Krashen (1981, 1985). Drawing on his acquisition–learning distinction, Krashen (1981) suggests that aptitude is relevant for learning only, and for classrooms, since it requires conscious focus and rule isolation. There are essentially three parts to the analysis of the claim that Krashen makes. These are (a) to consider the underlying model, since, if the model is inadequate, the force of the criticism is reduced, (b) to consider the logical relationship between the model and the functioning of aptitude in formal and informal situations, and (c) to consider the empirical evidence that is available. The first of these considerations is beyond the scope of the present volume, but the Monitor Model has come under some searching criticism, starting with McLaughlin (1978), through more recent critiques in Gregg (1984), and Skehan (1984a), and finally McLaughlin (1987). These suggest that the acquisition–learning distinction has not been sustained either theoretically or empirically, so that the basis for the attack on aptitude loses force.

To examine the logical relationship between aptitude and context of learning, it is useful to recall the three-component view of aptitude, i.e. that it consists of phonemic coding ability, language analytic ability, and memory. We need now to examine the relevance of each of these for informal learning situations. Krashen (1981) proposed that the language analytic capacity cannot be used on naturalistic input, and on unfocused language where teaching is not involved. But there is nothing within any theory of aptitude to require that this should be the case. It is just as likely that such a capacity should operate in all situations, focused or unfocused, conscious or unconscious. In each case linguistic processing is involved, and some sort of target language system results. With formal learning the linguistic material is laid out in the manner meant to be most helpful for the learner to engage his language learning capacities. In informal settings there is less preliminary organization so the learner has a considerably greater problem in imposing structure on the data. Yet the target, the structure to be imposed, is the same, so it is arguable that language analytic capacities, as conceived within aptitude research, are even *more* important.

The second component of aptitude to be considered is that of phonemic coding ability. Cognitive psychologists (e.g. Lindsay and Norman 1977) make a distinction between 'top-down' and 'bottom-up' processing. The former arises when the comprehender uses schematic knowledge (Widdowson 1983) to project onto the input data their likely content, i.e. prediction is the starting point for comprehension which is confirmed through a 'stimulus sampling' cycle. Bottom-up processing, on the other hand, is more stimulus-bound, in that the actual stimulus material is examined more thoroughly, on an element-by-element basis. Quite clearly, on-going comprehension is a mixture of top-down and bottom-up processing. Top-down processing is limited by some need to sample the stimulus material: bottom-up processing is limited, amongst other reasons, by the need to process language in real-time. So speech comprehension is a mixture of the two processes, with the balance depending on things like task demands (e.g. familiarity) and ID variables (e.g. processing capacities). It seems probable that *foreign* language processing is more reliant on a bottom-up approach, and that therefore phonemic coding ability will be involved. In formal situations one probably gets the greatest degree of message adjustment to take account of learner limitations, so that the phonemic coding abilities of the learners will, if the teacher can achieve this, be equalized out. In contrast, in informal situations, there is likely to be less message adjustment. Some negotiation of meaning can, of course, take place (Long 1983b), but this will be variable and undependable. So those capacities which reduce the need for such adjustments will put the learner at an advantage. Hence the relevance of phonemic coding ability for *all* contexts of learning.

We come next to memory. Here two contrasting viewpoints each need to be considered. First, one may view language acquisition as the growth of a grammatical system, with a complementary and subservient need to learn vocabulary. Alternatively, one can make even stronger claims here if one accepts the arguments of linguists such as Bolinger (1975) and Pawley and Syder (1983) who suggest that actual language data (as opposed to contrived examples) are nothing like as rule governed as linguists suggest. In reality language and language use are heavily dependent on memory systems, which in turn rely to a considerable extent on prefabricated and idiomatic language. If this second viewpoint is accepted, there is an even more enlarged role for memory, since it suggests that language development consists of the acquisition of, and control over, more and more language 'chunks', implying a retrieval system of enormous scale and complexity. And once again, there is no reason to think that informal settings are less dependent on the memory component of aptitude than are formal ones. In each case, high-level functioning in the target language will require the assimilation of a considerable quantity of material. So we see that each of the components of aptitude can be logically related to informal as well as formal learning situations.

Finally, we need to consider the empirical evidence. Only one relevant study has been located. Reves (1983) investigated the role of several potential predictors of language learning success, i.e. aptitude, motivation, cognitive style, and learning strategies, in two situations – one formal and one informal. The informal setting involved the acquisition of Hebrew by L1 Arabic speakers in Israel while the formal setting was of the *same group* learning English under classroom conditions. Thus the one set of subjects acted as its own control. Reves found essentially that prediction was less effective in the formal learning environment, with generally lower levels of correlation between the single predictors and criterion measures. This is an unsurprising result since there is less standardization of learning conditions in the informal situation, and it is more likely that extraneous influences will reduce the contribution of single predictors. What is most interesting, though, is to consider the interaction between the predictors and the learning settings. In the informal situation, it was *aptitude* that was the most effective predictor of language learning success, confirming the claim made earlier in this section that the constellation of skills tapped by aptitude batteries are relevant to settings which do not involve instruction as well as those which do. In contrast, the other predictors, despite the claims made for them (e.g. Gardner 1985 on motivation), faded in importance, generating quite low correlations (see Skehan 1986a for more discussion of these results).

5: Aptitude test measures are not 'pure' measures, and only achieve prediction, not explanation:

It is possible that the existing aptitude tests do not, in fact, measure the constructs underlying language aptitude, but rather qualities only indirectly related to them. There is the possibility that aptitude tests achieve their prediction because they function as surrogate measures of other qualities, e.g. test-wiseness or intelligence, and it is these other qualities which account for the 'aptitude'–criterion correlations. Basically this criticism exists at two levels. The more superficial of these would account for the correlations between aptitude and criterion tests in terms of test format effects. Consider, for example, the situation where a paper-and-pencil based multiple-choice test, e.g. the Words in Sentences sub-test from the MLAT, correlates with a paper-and-pencil multiple-choice criterion test. The cause of the correlation may be at least partly test-taking ability at Time 1 correlating with test-taking ability at Time 2. A convincing response to this criticism is not easy to give. It would, basically, require the demonstration, through a multitrait–multimethod design and the establishment of divergent validity, that it is the *constructs* concerned that are correlating. Since such a comprehensive research study has not been done, we need to consider several supporting lines of argument. There is the role of theory, covered earlier, in justifying the constructs concerned. In addition, one can draw inferences from various studies which do demonstrate a selective and superior effect for aptitude. Some of the studies relating intelligence tests to language learning success are of this sort, since the intelligence tests contain similar formats to the aptitude tests, but are surpassed by them. The Bristol research also supports the contention that aptitude tests measure more than test-taking ability since the correlations include some with indices, e.g. of syntax and vocabulary, derived from naturalistic data. There is also the reassurance that aptitude has different components that relate to one another in predictable ways. This constitutes some degree of discriminant validation for the constructs concerned.

Another angle on this same problem is to look at the criterion measures that the aptitude tests are correlated with. Krashen (1981a) proposes that aptitude tests only correlate with non-communicative measures of performance or with 'learning' as opposed to 'acquisition' type tests. Now it is certainly true that many criterion tests used in aptitude research have been of an 'objective', multiple-choice format. However, this has merely reflected the general wisdom on testing. As it happens, the changes in testing since 1970 (see Davies 1978, and Skehan in press c for reviews) have coincided with much less aptitude research being done. What research has been carried out suggests that when more communicative tests are used, predictive validity coefficients are still significant and substantial. Skehan (1982), for example, using criterion tests of translating, interpreting, and conversation, reported correlations frequently above 0.40. Similarly the Bristol longitudinal research found aptitude–achievement correlations in excess of 0.50 and even above 0.70, in the context of the NFER/APU tests (Dickson *et al*. 1985) which are indeed claimed to be communicative. Finally, much of the aptitude research conducted in the American Armed Forces used the FSI test, which does indeed assess communicative performance. Thus one can certainly point to aptitude studies where sizable correlations are found, even though communicative criterion tests are used, and where the test form of the aptitude tests is quite different from that of the criterion tests.

There is, however, a more searching version of the 'format effect' criticism. This is that aptitude tests are hybrid measures of aptitude constructs, on the one hand, and decontextualized language abilities, on the other. We saw the importance of decontextualization abilities when evaluating the Bristol follow-up research, where aptitude test performance was predicted by early measures of first language syntax *and* by measures reflecting early emerging decontextualization abilities. This may also be what Neufeld (1978) means when he talks about the distinction between primary and secondary abilities. It is possible that performance on aptitude tests is partly dependent on a decontextualization ability, and only partly on aptitude constructs themselves. The tests often require multiple-choice performance and skills that have to be used without any obvious contextual cueing. It could be that some learners who have problems in coping with the *test*-based measures of these aptitudinal capacities would cope more effectively with exposure to similar material in more natural contexts. Similarly, performance on criterion measures might reflect not simply proficiency in the target language, but also the capacity to see what is required by the test format concerned.

In fact, the influence of decontextualization abilities may be even more fundamental than simply to affect test performance: *language teaching itself* may be part of the problem. Teachers, to achieve efficiency and generality, may use the classroom as a condensed version of the way language is used outside, in the hope that the more concentrated exposure provided will be later exploited in a wide range of situations. A version of this approach underlies grammar-based teaching, where learners are exposed to a diet of structures and grammar points which they are meant to draw upon, as needed, in real life. It is for the learner to perceive the indirect relationship between what happens in class and outside. To a certain extent, with communicative approaches, there is more concern to provide opportunities for language use, to develop communication strategies, to encourage the negotiation of meaning. The problem, however, is that while the degree of decontextualization has been reduced, decontextualization itself has not been removed. Activities such as information-gap activities (one-way or two-way), role plays, simulations, primed discussions and the like do provide the learner with purposes for communication, but they are not the learner's own purposes, or the outgrowth of the learner's own life. Nor are the participants in the activities in such classrooms identical to the participants the learner will actually converse with. In the classroom the learner is not really given much opportunity to interact with people with whom there is shared knowledge, who achieve communication as an interplay between what each of them knows about what the other does or does not know.

So this criticism of aptitude research is, rather disappointingly, not without foundation. However, if we are realistic, it is unusual indeed to find practical measures which are indeed transparent measures of the underlying constructs. What is more important, in fact, is to know what components underlie any actual measure, so that, blended as these may be, we at least know what is being measured, and can make judgements based on this knowledge.

Language aptitude, SLA, and models of communicative competence

In the previous sections the discussion has focused on aptitude research within its own terms, and has concluded that the concept of aptitude is still an important one. This final section, in contrast, will go outside this framework, and draw upon later insights into the process and aims of language learning. There will be two themes. The first will consider the relevance for aptitude of recent trends in second language acquisition: the second will similarly examine the nature of communicative competence.

A great deal of effort in SLA has concerned the way in which input is processed. We saw, in an earlier section on phonemic coding ability, how the distinction between bottom-up and top-down processing can fruitfully be applied to aptitude research. At the lowest level we have the discrimination–segmentation problem, where learners have to impose some structure on the sounds that they hear. Peters (1983) argues that this is immensely important in determining the sort of input that becomes available for any linguistic analysis and we saw how phonemic coding ability is relevant for this. It is possible that even greater attention to the auditory aspects of language learning might lead to an extension of the sub-tests available in this area, as the psycho-linguistic problems involved in segmenting the speech stream become better understood.

Moving to more central processes in the handling of input, we can consider the difficulties posed for learners by complex form–function or function–form relationships during the learning of a foreign language. Recently Sato (1985) and Huebner (1985) have shown how learners have difficulty coping with situations where one form in the target language is used to express more than one function or where more than one function will be expressed by one form. It is possible that some learners are more able to deal with confusing input of this sort than others. This may be influenced by aptitude constructs such as grammatical sensitivity and inductive language learning ability, but this connection is far from clear. There is scope to explore the importance of such language learning processes for underlying aptitudes, to see whether 'new' aptitudes are involved. The same is true for the 'processes' discussed within SLA. Long (in press) enumerates here language transfer, overgeneralization, simplification, fossilization, nativization, denativization, pidginization, and creolization. Each process seems to regard as beneficial the capacity to make hypotheses, and then to be able to restructure verbal knowledge in the light of the feedback that is received. It seems certain that there will be individual differences here both in the capacity to generate hypotheses as well as to modify current linguistic structures. It would seem sensible, therefore, that these differences should be investigated as part of an extended construct of aptitude.

Finally, if we consider the top-down nature of language processing, we need to recognize that a great deal of comprehension is achieved not simply through the actual language being received, but by the interpretative capacities of the listener (Widdowson 1983). Conversational implicatures are made (Levinson 1983) and schematic knowledge is used to make sense of current events (Widdowson 1983). Consider, as in the following passage, what happens when we are deprived of these interpretative capacities:

> Sally first tried setting loose a team of gophers. The plan backfired when a dog chased them away. She then entertained a group of teenagers and was delighted when they brought their motorcycles. Unfortunately, she failed to find a Peeping Tom listed in the Yellow Pages. Furthermore, her stereo system was not loud enough. The crab grass might have worked but she didn't have a fan that was sufficiently powerful. The obscene phone calls gave her hope until the number was changed. She thought about calling a door-to-door salesman but decided to hang up a clothesline instead. It was the installation of blinking neon lights across the street that did the trick. She eventually framed the ad from the classified section. (Bransford *et. al.*, cited in Urquart 1984, p. 32)

Most readers will initially respond to this passage with great difficulty since there is no obvious frame of reference. The reader/listener is forced into a bottom-up mode of processing, and deprived of any straightforward and satisfactory way of making predictions. Even when this text is given to native speakers enormous individual differences manifest themselves. A few spot the 'subject' in no time, but others totally fail to see that the text is about getting rid of noisy neighbours.

This discussion brings out two important claims – that accessing relevant schematic knowledge and discourse capacities is extremely facilitating for comprehension; and that people vary in how readily they can do this. The implication is that it would be extremely useful to devise aptitude tests to assess how effectively learners can mobilize such knowledge as an aid to general understanding, i.e. how efficiently they can convert input into some sort of intake. It implies, that is, three levels of receptive processing:

1 Input: Everything that impinges on the learner
2 Comprehension Intake: Everything which is understood, by whatever means. Much schematically driven comprehension will be at this level.

3 Linguistic Intake: Everything which can, retrospectively or instantly, be processed linguistically, including that which may require slight extension of current linguistic competence for processing.

The difference between (1) and the other levels is now commonplace, following Corder's (1973) original input/intake distinction. The distinction between (2) and (3) is not always made however. It is made here as it clarifies that the role of schematic knowledge in language comprehension may often be at level (2). In such cases there may not be any great force for linguistic change (although aspects of language such as vocabulary may be developed) but the learner will avoid becoming disengaged from the thread of discourse, and still be ready for examples of (3) linguistic intake, when they present themselves. And it is these which are the real growth points for language (Swain 1985, Skehan 1987). This presents something of a dilemma for aptitude research and theorizing. It currently has a bias towards an information processing perspective, and to the way in which *input* is handled. Yet there is increasing work on the role of interaction in learning (Pica, Doughty and Young 1986; Day 1986) and the importance of production and communication strategies for long-term growth (Faerch and Kasper 1983). Current models of aptitude do not cover these areas so well. To a certain extent this is not a problem exclusive to aptitude research, since the comprehension–production relationship is not at all well handled in applied linguistics. However, if aptitude tests are to reflect how language is used as well as how it is processed, it would be desirable for them to have a greater emphasis on interaction and production.

The second general area for the extension of language aptitude research concerns the nature of communicative competence. Aptitude research has only been concerned with *linguistic* competence, and with the learner's capacity to handle sentence grammar. Contemporary views on competence are more likely to incorporate Hymes's (1970) discussion of *communicative* competence, which, in addition to including whether something is formally possible, considers whether it is appropriate, whether it is feasible psychologically, and whether it is done. Canale and Swain (1980) and Canale (1983), building on Hymes's work (1970), propose a model of communicative competence which draws on four component competences: linguistic, sociolinguistic, discourse, and strategic.

The Canale and Swain model implies there are stable aptitudes which predispose some learners to acquire competences other than the linguistic. For sociolinguistic competence such aptitudes would probably concern a sensitivity by some people to appropriate language use and social norms. For discourse competence, research would need to identify whether some learners are able to make their spoken or written language more coherent and cohesive, and whether some people are predisposed to manage conversations more effectively. Finally, for strategic competence, one would have to investigate whether some learners are more able to improvise and to use language creatively, and whether such linguistic capacity has favourable consequences for long-term language development as opposed to merely solving temporary problems.

This 'agenda' is clearly demanding. It seems likely that many of the capacities that are important for the development of sociolinguistic, discourse, and strategic competence are different from those which underlie aptitudinal constructs which predict linguistic competence. They are more likely to be based in personality or social style. Such IDs will be discussed in later chapters, since we may be dealing with the willingness different learners have to talk in order to learn, and this, as a non-cognitive ID, may be altogether more elusive for researchers. However, some of the aptitudes concerned, especially those involving the cognitive dimensions of being able to handle extended discourse, make appropriate conversational implicatures, and generally make sense of on-going discourse through the use of schematic knowledge, may be eminently investigable by conventional aptitude methodologies. One can conclude, then, by saying that considerable progress has already been made in foreign language aptitude research, but that there are several interesting areas for future investigation.

4

Motivation

Corder's phrase, 'Given motivation, anyone can learn a language' brings out the importance of motivation and the way it can overcome unfavourable circumstances in other aspects of language learning. However, the definition and study of motivation have not been without their problems, so that demonstrating its effects has been far from simple. This chapter will address the issue of motivation in five main sections. It will start with a layman's or 'naive' view of the problem, followed by a discussion of general psychological viewpoints on motivation. The third section of the chapter is concerned with earlier and contemporary views of *specific* motivations for language study, and in particular, the work of Robert Gardner. The fourth simultaneously evaluates Gardner's work and discusses the major issues in the study of motivation. The final section attempts to relate the findings on individual differences in motivation to a wider educational framework.

A layman's approach to motivation

Motivation can, in principle, have several sources. One such source might be the learning activity itself (the Intrinsic Hypothesis). In such cases the stimulus for motivation would be the inherent interest of learning, because classrooms or learning situations might be attractive places in themselves. Alternatively motivation might be influenced by the success experienced by learners (the Resultative hypothesis). Those learners who do well experience reward, and are encouraged to try harder: learners who do not do so well are discouraged by their lack of success, and, as a result, lack persistence. Motivation would be a consequence rather than a cause of success. The individual may also 'bring' to the learning situation a certain quantity of motivation as a 'given', leading to the interesting question of why an individual is motivated to

	Within the learning context	The results of learning
Outside the individual	Materials Teaching	Constraints, Rewards
Inside the individual	Success	Goals

Figure 4.1: Dimensions of motivational sources

the degree that he or she is (the 'Internal Cause' hypothesis). Finally, there may be external influences and incentives, such as rewards contingent upon the learner succeeding or sanctions which influence performance (the 'Carrot and Stick' hypothesis).

The four sources of motivation can be arranged in the form of a 2-by-2 matrix to clarify their interrelationships, as in Figure 4.1. The upper row covers *influences* upon students' motivation which may be manipulated by external factors. These influences could be the use of materials and activities with greater inherent interest, or the involvement of more inspiring and stimulating teachers. They could also involve the use of frequent tests and examinations, or the provision of reward for learning. In contrast, the lower row emphasizes the role of the individual. Within the learning context, this concerns the success that is achieved, and the effects this has on motivational levels. Outside the learning context, we focus more on the goals that the learner may have to sustain the efforts required for learning. And it is this area, which relates to ID research, and the influence of goals on motivational levels, that will be emphasized in the present chapter. The purpose of the matrix is to remind us of the wider framework within which motivational forces operate.

General psychological approaches to motivation

We will consider two general approaches to motivation: Need Achievement Theory, and Attribution Theory.

Need achievement theory

McClelland *et al.* (1953) suggested that different levels of the need to achieve (nAch) are the result of previous learning experiences. 'Achievers' are those people who, on the basis of previous learning experiences, perceive new learning situations and problems as outside their present capabilities, but attainable with some effort. They are people, that is, who expect the world to contain reasonable challenges, and respond to such challenges. In contrast, low achievers are people whose previous learning experiences are discouraging and unsuccessful. McClelland (1953) proposes that such people prefer challenges and tasks which are either excessively demanding, or very easy. The justification for this counter-intuitive prediction is that in the first case, failure is bearable, and the second, very unlikely.

The nAch concept has been criticized within psychology primarily on empirical grounds. This is because nAch has not been found to improve the prediction of *academic* success, suggesting that the drive to achieve, if it exists, must be at a fairly generalized level. There have also been claims that achievement in learning situations may be dependent on the subject involved, with different motivational patterns appropriate to different disciplines (Jones *et al*. 1973), and also that different patterns of motivation may be sex-linked (Mehrabian 1968). The nAch construct has not been used extensively in language learning studies, but when it has, it has not produced high levels of correlation (Gardner and Lambert 1972).

Attribution theory
Psychologists (e.g. Brown 1986, Greene 1985) have, in recent years turned their attention to attribution theory. Such theories view as fundamental the way people attribute causes to events, and suggest that people vary in the way they do this. The basic contrasts are shown in Figure 4.2.

| | Locus of control | |
	Internal	External
Stable	Ability	Task difficulty
Unstable	Effort	Luck

Figure 4.2: An attributional analysis of causes

Four basic causes of achievement are postulated: ability; task difficulty; effort, and luck. These are analysed along two dimensions: stability and locus of control. The stability dimension contrasts ability and task difficulty, both of which are thought to be relatively unmodifiable, with effort and luck, each of which may possibly change on another attempt to perform a task. The locus of control dimension contrasts causes which reside within the individual (ability and effort) and causes which are outside (task difficulty and luck). In principle, people may attribute causes to any of these four factors. In practice people may be systematic in what they view to be important causally. Brown (1986) discusses evidence that there are systematic styles in how attributions are made, and how generally attributions are thought to apply. Some people are more disposed to an 'effort' interpretation, others more to an 'ability' explanation. Some people are more wide-ranging while others judge causes only in relation to specific situations. Worst of all, some people, in a vicious double-bind, consistently attribute bad outcomes to stable (i.e. unmodifiable) attributes, and good outcomes to unstable causes, i.e. the bad will always recur, but the good may not. Studies within education which have compared these two dimensions of locus of control and stability have suggested that it is stability which is more important (Greene 1985), and that perceiving success (or failure) as being dependent on the relatively fixed factors of ability (Greene 1985) or task difficulty is likely to influence expectations of future performance more than when effort or luck are thought to be important.

Clearly what is important for language learning are the causative factors to which success is ascribed. If the stable factors of ability (intelligence and language aptitude) and the inherent difficulty of language learning are thought to be important, then persistence will be lower. If, on the other hand, unstable factors such as effort and luck are psychologically prominent, persistence and motivation will be higher since the learner will see himself as having a potential impact on learning progress. Whatever the individual's post-learning experiences may be, the main measurement problem here is the need to assess learner beliefs about the causes of learning success. It would be desirable if more attribution theory research were carried out in the language learning field. Such research might even synthesize many of the IDs discussed in this book into a more coherent account of language learning.

Specific motivations for language learning

Early theories

We turn next to research which assumes that there is a motivation specific to language study. Far and away the most important work done in this area has been by Robert Gardner (earlier with Wallace Lambert, and later with research associates at the University of Western Ontario). The original theory was an outgrowth of Mowrer's views (1950) on individual development which emphasize the importance of identification with a valued person. Gardner and Lambert (1959, 1972) built on this idea and considered the extent to which people esteem and want to identify with not only particular individuals but also foreign peoples. Variation in these factors was thought to be the result of attitudes towards foreigners which were probably formed under the influence of parents, the home environment, and the native culture.

Gardner and Lambert (1972) suggested that those people who identify positively in this way would like to resemble the foreign peoples concerned, to understand their culture, and to be able to participate in it. This pattern of motivation they label an *integrative orientation*. It is a particularly important source of motivation because it is firmly based in the personality of the learner. As such it is likely to exert its influence over an extended period and to sustain learning efforts over the time that is necessary to attain language learning success.

Gardner and Lambert (1972) also described an *instrumental orientation* to language learning. This type of motivation is based on the advantages that can accrue if a language is known, e.g. professional advancement; capacity to do one's job well; ability to read useful material in the target language; potential to exploit members of the foreign culture, etc. Gardner and Lambert hypothesized that an instrumental motive is less effective because it is not rooted in the personality of the learner, and therefore, more dependent on fallible external pressures. As a result, the learner is less likely to expend effort to achieve cumulative progress.

The Gardner and Lambert theory generated an enormous quantity of research. Groups of language learners were administered extensive test

Table 4.1: The factors from the early Gardner–Lambert research

	Montreal	Louisiana	Connecticut	Philippines
Factor 1	Language aptitude/ French achievement (standardised tests)	IQ/Language aptitude/ French achievement (standardised tests)	IQ/Language aptitude/ French achievement (standardised tests)	English achievement/ Language aptitude (one sub-test)
Factor 2	Motivational orientation/ Motivational intensity/ French achievement	French achievement (oral ability)	Parental attitudes to learning French	Gen. motivation/ Study habits/ English achievement (oral skills- partly)
Factor 3	Attitudes to learning French	Attitudes to learning French	French achievement (oral ability)/ Language aptitude	Parental Instrumental orientation/ English achievement

Note: In each case only the first three factors have been examined, since they are the most important ones. In addition, the labelling of factors is that of the present author, not Gardner and Lambert's.

batteries containing (a) measures of motivation, (b) measures of aptitude, and (c) achievement measures. The resulting data matrix was then subjected to factor analysis and the pattern of loadings inspected. The hypotheses were that factors would emerge with loadings on *both* the causal variables, e.g. aptitude or integrative motivation, *and* the criterion variables. The results obtained, typically, were somewhat confirmatory of the Gardner–Lambert position, but not universally so. A summary of several research studies is presented in Table 4.1.

The Montreal study provides the clearest evidence in support of the original hypothesis. The first two factors are hybrid, as predicted, indicating a relationship between aptitude and achievement (Factor One), and motivational orientation and achievement (Factor Two). The other studies, however, are less supportive. In both Louisiana and Connecticut a hybrid aptitude–achievement factor emerges, but achievement (oral ability) and attitudes generate *separate* factors. The Philippines study is more complex to interpret. There is limited evidence for the role of aptitude in achievement, some evidence linking general motivation to an oral ability dimension of achievement; and evidence linking a *parental instrumental* motivation to a range of English achievement measures.

The general conclusion from this early research is that there is some evidence in support of the Gardner–Lambert (1972) position, but other data which are not so favourable. As a generalization, one could say that the clearly bilingual setting of Montreal provides confirming results; the less bilingual American settings show evidence of attitudinal factors not clearly linked to achievement; and the Philippines study links achievement with a more generalized motivation (Factor 2) or parental instrumental motivation. In Montreal, this would imply that learning French is associated with wanting to be like French Canadians while in the Philippines learning English is associated with wanting to be able to use English. In any case, we can conclude that these early studies contained considerable promise; that they made important progress in the development of measurement techniques and that they were worth pursuing.

Contemporary research into a specific FL motivation

Conceptualizing specific motivations

Gardner (1985) now proposes that the following equation can be used to represent the components of motivation:

$$\text{Motivation} = \textit{Effort} + \textit{Desire to Achieve a Goal} + \textit{Attitudes} \qquad 4.1$$

Motivation is made up, first, of effort, but as Gardner points out (1985, p.10), there are several potential components of effort, such as compulsiveness, desire to please a teacher or parent, a high need to achieve, good study habits, social pressures, including examinations or external rewards, which do not relate specifically to learning a language. Gardner, in other words, is suggesting that it is important to study what channels this effort. Moving to the right-hand side of the equation, attitudes are:

> an evaluative reaction to some referent or attitude object, inferred on the basis of the individual's beliefs or opinions about the referent. (Gardner 1985, p.9)

As Gardner goes on to say:

> The accumulated evidence in the area of second language acquisition indicates that attitudes are related to behaviour, though not necessarily directly.

We see, then, that attitudes are thought of as the sustaining base for the middle term in the equation, the desire to achieve a goal, which is the place at which an integrative orientation is important. It is here that the particular goal that is involved, language learning in this case, and the particular viewpoint on it, integrative orientation, shapes the direction for the motivation to operate.

We need next to examine the measuring instrument generally used by Gardner and his associates. This is the Attitude Motivation Index (AMI). It consists of eleven measures. These are (for French in Canada as the target language: other target languages would need to be substituted for other situations):

1 Attitude to French-speaking Canadians
2 Attitudes to European French people
3 Interest in foreign languages
4 Integrative orientation
5 Motivational intensity
6 Desire to learn French
7 Attitudes towards learning French
8 French teaching – evaluative
9 French course – evaluative
10 Instrumental orientation
11 French class anxiety

The first 10 measures are added together; and then the score for the eleventh, French class anxiety, is subtracted from this total. By doing this, Gardner is clearly taking a simple additive model to obtain a composite measure of motivation. The different attitudinal measures (1, 2, 3, 7, 8, 9), the different orientation indices (4, 10), and the indices of effort (5, 6) are simply added, unweighted, with the additional construct of anxiety, since it is assumed to be debilitating (see Chapter 6 for more extensive discussion of this construct), subtracted from the total. This seems a disappointingly simple measurement technique, given the complexity and subtlety of the theorizing that led up to it.

Empirical research
There are three major types of evidence on the relationships that the AMI enters into. These are:

1 with achievement
2 with perseverance
3 with classroom behaviour and acquisitional processes

Relationships with achievement can be covered best by examining a typical study. Gardner (1980) examined the correlations between the Attitude Motivation Index (AMI), the Modern Languages Aptitude Test (MLAT), and French grades, for a large number of different locations and secondary school ages. A sample of the results is shown in Table 4.2. The original data in Gardner (1980) are based on seven different geographical areas. Two have been chosen here as representative. Area One yields slightly higher correlations than average; Area Four lower. Quite clearly the AMI is a significant and consistent correlate of grades, and the median correlation of 0.37 indicates (in the circumstances) a fairly impressive level of relationship. It demonstrates that what is measured by the AMI is certainly relevant to foreign language achievement, and to that extent the hypotheses put forward by Gardner have received support. It is interesting that the MLAT also generated comparable correlations with grades. Equally interesting is the third

Table 4.2: Correlations amongst AMI, MLAT, and French grades

	AMI × Grades	MLAT × Grades	AMI × MLAT	Multiple correlation
Area 1				
Grade 8	.37**	.44**	.06	.56
Grade 9	.46**	.30**	.21*	.51
Grade 10	.42**	.43**	.04	.59
Grade 11	.43**	.59**	.23*	.66
Area 2				
Grade 7	.34**	.24**	.09	.40
Grade 8	.32**	.32**	.15	.42
Grade 9	.38**	.40**	.17*	.51
Grade 10	.28**	.41**	− .04	.51
Grade 11	.45**	.48**	.20*	.60
Median (all seven areas)	.37	.41	.13	.52

** = $p < .01$ * = $p < .05$

column – the correlations between the AMI and the MLAT. The median correlation here is only 0.13, suggesting at best a tenuous relationship between the two measures since such a correlation might be attributable to a method effect. As a result the two independent variables combine well, and the multiple correlation represents quite a jump on either one taken singly. The median multiple correlation of 0.52 suggests an impressive amount of the variance in the criterion scores has been accounted for.

The second strand of evidence on the effects of motivation concerns perseverance in language study. Several studies (Bartley 1969, 1970; Clement *et al.* 1978) suggest that it is motivational factors which are most implicated in cases where students drop out of language study, and which are most predictive of those who will drop out. However, although attitudinal and motivational indices have been regularly demonstrated to be potent influences at a global level, there has been little consistency in which aspects of the AMI are the basis for the relationships found.

There have also been studies relating motivational characteristics to classroom behaviour and acquisitional processes. Gliksman (1976), for example, has shown that students classified as having integrative orientations to language study volunteered more frequently in class, were asked more questions by the teacher when not volunteering, gave more correct answers, and received more positive reinforcement from the teacher than those without this motivation orientation. We should bear in mind here that motivation has been shown to be independent of aptitude, so that the above results are not simply a disguised correlation of ability with behaviour. Nor, since there was no interaction with the length of the course, is there evidence of success being the causal variable which is feeding back and raising levels of motivation among those who are making favourable progress (see discussion of this point below). Naiman *et al.* (1978) produced comparable results although in their case there does not seem to be a selective effect for *integrative* orientation, since positive correlations were found between student handraising (as the measure of classroom participation), and indices of not only integrative orientation but also instrumental orientation, motivation, and evaluation of the means of learning French. A specifically integrative motive was involved in a study by Kaplan and Shand (1984) who argue that such an orientation is related to systematic patterns of error detection, which could well have implications for error correction and subsequent language development. This would be consistent with the distinction Meisel (1980) makes between segregative and integrative orientations. The former, which obviously leads learners to keep social distance from the target language group, is associated with a language learning strategy of 'restrictive' simplification which involves the omission of syntactic and morphological elements, and a more

pidginized form of communication. An integrative orientation is associated with an elaborative simplification strategy, i.e. hypothesis
formation about the target language and a willingness to restructure the
linguistic system. Meisel (1980) proposes that this strategy is associated
with greater progress. Similarly, in terms of acquisitional processes,
Gardner, Lalonde, and Moorcroft (1985) have shown that the AMI is
related to speed of learning of paired-associate vocabulary.

An educational model

Quite clearly, the evidence considered so far, mostly correlational,
represents a fairly low level of theorizing. Essentially bivariate relationships are involved, and relatively few of them at that. One is only looking at a limited section of the 'taxonomy model' discussed in Chapter 1,
and the extensive accumulation of data has been more consistent with a
'research-then-theory' perspective, although the more recent acquisi-
tion-process studies are an exception to this. Gardner has however
(1985) developed a more extensive and ambitious model, as shown in
Figure 4.3. It is easiest to consider this model right-to-left. The right-
most column distinguishes between linguistic and non-linguistic outcomes. The next column to the left, Second Language Acquisition
Contexts, differentiates between formal and informal language training, i.e. between explicit instruction in schools, and uninstructed
acquisition-oriented settings outside classrooms. These two contexts of
instruction are thought to be influenced by four ID variables since aptitude and motivation are supplemented by two others, intelligence and
situational anxiety. The broken lines joining intelligence and aptitude
with informal language learning contrast with the solid lines joining
them to formal settings. This reflects the hypothesis put forward by
Gardner that there is a weaker connection for these two variables when
informal contexts are concerned, while motivation and situational
anxiety are posited to influence both learning contexts equally.

The final component of the model is the social milieu in which the
individual is situated, and in which attitudes and expectations are
formed. Gardner (1979) proposes that expectations about bilingualism
as well as attitudes towards the target language and its community are
the basis for attitudes towards language learning. Essentially, as far as
the social milieu–motivation connection is concerned, this is where the
equation proposed earlier fits into the model, i.e. motivation is a function of effort plus desire to attain a goal plus attitudes.

The schematic model shown in Figure 4.3 is reformulated in operational terms in Figure 4.4. Intelligence and situational anxiety do not
appear in this second model. Further, language aptitude is given an
autonomous position, without the rather odd foundation in social
milieu. With one exception, the rest of the model is a stripped-down

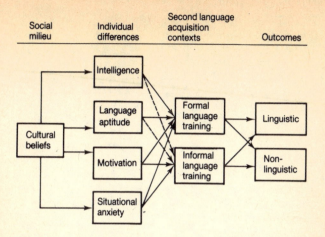

Figure 4.3: The Gardner educational model (after Gardner 1985)

version of the original. The exception is that there is greater specification of the linkages involving motivation. Integrativeness and attitudes towards the learning situation are rooted in the social milieu, and influence motivation which, in turn, influences achievement in all acquisition contexts (unlike aptitude, which is again downgraded to influence directly only the formal contexts).

Figure 4.4 implies chains of causation, and to address this issue, Gardner has pioneered the use of complex statistical procedures in language learning research. He has used causal modelling techniques (Gardner 1985, pp.156–66), and LISREL in particular (see discussion in

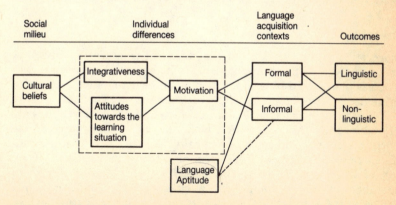

Figure 4.4: Operational formulation of the socio-educational model (after Gardner 1985)

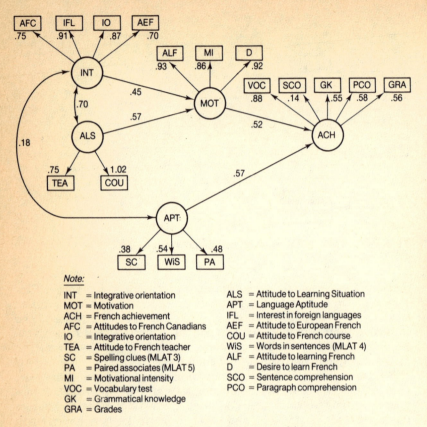

Figure 4.5: Causal modelling of foreign language achievement

Note:

INT	= Integrative orientation	
MOT	= Motivation	
ACH	= French achievement	
AFC	= Attitudes to French Canadians	
IO	= Integrative orientation	
TEA	= Attitude to French teacher	
SC	= Spelling clues (MLAT 3)	
PA	= Paired associates (MLAT 5)	
MI	= Motivational intensity	
VOC	= Vocabulary test	
GK	= Grammatical knowledge	
GRA	= Grades	

ALS	= Attitude to Learning Situation
APT	= Language Aptitude
IFL	= Interest in foreign languages
AEF	= Attitude to European French
COU	= Attitude to French course
WiS	= Words in sentences (MLAT 4)
ALF	= Attitude to learning French
D	= Desire to learn French
SCO	= Sentence comprehension
PCO	= Paragraph comprehension

Chapter 2), to try to tease out the chains of causation involved. A typical analysis is shown in Figure 4.5. where each of the central constructs is represented by a large circle, with the actual measures which define the construct represented by the small boxes. The measures are related to the constructs by loadings, which indicate how well they are defined by the various measures, while the causal paths between the constructs are also indicated numerically. We see, then, that the construct of achievement (ACH) is accounted for by motivation (MOT), with a loading of 0.52, and aptitude (APT), with a loading of 0.57. In turn, motivation is accounted for by integrativeness (INT) through a loading of 0.45, and Attitude towards the Learning Situation (ALS), with a loading of 0.57.

At a greater level of detail, and moving away from the causal links between the constructs, each construct is defined by various measures. Integrativeness has high loadings on Attitudes to French Canadians, Interest in Foreign Languages, Integrative Orientation, and Attitudes towards European French, while Attitudes towards the Learning Situation loads highly on Teacher Evaluation and French Course Evaluation. Aptitude has high loadings on three sub-tests in the short form of the MLAT, and achievement has high loadings on four out of five tests (vocabulary, grammar, paragraph comprehension and grades, but not on sentence comprehension). Finally, motivation is well defined by Attitudes towards Learning French, Motivational Intensity, and Desire to Learn French. The final test for a causal model of this form is whether it fits the data well. This is evaluated by means of a X^2 analysis. Gardner (1985, p.159) reports a goodness-of-fit statistic of 131.12, which, at the appropriate degrees of freedom (109) is not significant, suggesting that the causal model has made predictions which are consistent with the data, and the underlying theories have been supported.

The influence of motivation on language learning: a review of the issues

Without doubt, Gardner's work on the place of motivation in language learning is unique, and certainly its positive qualities far outweigh the negative. The level of theorizing is always high and his work has the virtues of making good connections with mainstream psychology as well as providing a relevant account of language learning. Almost all other writing on motivation therefore seems to be a commentary, in one way or another, on the agenda established by Gardner. In this section we will examine five areas which are relevant to *any* account of motivation in language learning. This will enable us to review the issue of motivation in general as well as evaluate Gardner's work specifically.

The problem of measuring motivation

Given the fundamental nature of Gardner's work on motivation, it is all the more striking that another investigator, John Oller, has claimed that Gardner's approach to measurement is invalid. Oller (1977; Oller and Perkins 1978a; Oller 1981) suggests that Gardner's measures correlate with language proficiency not because of the relationship between the underlying constructs (as Gardner hypothesizes), but because of the shared influences on the actual measuring devices of the approval motive, self-flattery, response set, and verbal intelligence. The approval motive (or the social desirability factor) is a danger for any sort of questionnaire or self-report data. The respondent may answer an item not with his true beliefs, attitudes, etc, but rather with the answer which he thinks will reflect well on him, i.e. the respondent works out what the 'good' or 'right' answer is, and gives it. Oller (Oller and Perkins 1978a) suggests that the approval motive is contaminating the attitude and motivation scales that Gardner uses. He (Oller 1981) also argues that self-flattery is an important influence, even accounting for 25 per cent of the shared variance. He bases this claim on a study (Oller and Perkins 1978a) reporting correlations between self-ratings on various personality traits, on the one hand, and ratings of value of the same traits, on the other. He reports higher correlations between (say) self-ratings of Outgoingness and valuations people make of Outgoingness as a general personality trait than between self-ratings of Outgoingness and 'general value' ratings of (say) Sociability. Oller and Perkins (1978a) interpret this to mean that people self-flatter by rating themselves higher on traits that they think are important, instead of attempting to be honest and objective. Further, Oller and Perkins (1978a) suggest that a positive response set may also account for some of the shared variance between attitude scales and language proficiency.

So far Oller's arguments have only concerned the attitude and motivation measures. In order to make his case Oller also has to demonstrate that the attitudinal and motivational measures share variance, because of these spurious influences, with the language proficiency measures. The chain of argument he uses here is that (a) language proficiency and intelligence tests have 64 per cent common variance, (b) first and second language proficiency tests are substantially correlated, (c) verbal intelligence is needed to understand the questions in attitude/motivation scales, (d) people who understand the questions are the ones who will be able to seek social approval, engage in self-flattery, and tell the difference between yes and no. Note that Oller is not simply arguing that subjects who take scales like the AMI in their L2 will draw upon language proficiency and verbal intelligence to self-flatter, etc.: he is also arguing that these same confounding variables influence those who take attitude scales in their L1. So Oller is suggesting that Gardner's correlations arise from the greater verbal intelligence of some subjects enabling them to (a) do well on proficiency tests, and (b) curry favour, to self-flatter, etc. on the AMI measures.

A series of facetious questions come to mind when faced with this argument. Do less intelligent people have difficulty flattering themselves? Do they have difficulty telling the difference between 'yes' and 'no'? Is a lack of intelligence in life compensated for by a greater personal objectivity? Did Einstein have tremendous fluency in Swahili? Can you be clever and not ingratiating? More seriously, there are serious problems with all stages of the argument that Oller has put forward. First of all, there is the issue of language proficiency. The premises of Oller's position have been vigourously attacked by language testing specialists. The articles by Carroll, Vollmer, and Farhady in Oller (1983) are already classics in rebutting any claims of a unitary competence hypothesis (Oller 1979), and others (e.g. Bachman and Palmer 1981) have demonstrated the multi-componential nature of language proficiency. In any case, the near-zero relationships between the AMI and the MLAT (which certainly does have some relationship to verbal intelligence (Wesche, Edwards and Wells 1982)) in itself rules out an intelligence 'explanation' of the AMI. There is no point in starting to argue, therefore, that verbal intelligence underlies foreign language proficiency – it quite clearly cannot, and the 64 per cent shared variance figure that Oller quotes is erroneous. The argument for a high correlation between first and second language proficiency is also defective. The studies that Oller quotes in support of this position mainly involve bilingual children. These findings can in no way be generalized to second and foreign language *learners*.

It is still possible, though, that attitudinal measures are influenced by factors such as the approval motive, etc. and are generally less effective measures as a result. The main empirical evidence that Oller uses for this argument is the study referred to earlier of correlations between self-ratings and general ratings of personality traits. The interpretation that Oller puts on the results is that people are flattering themselves about their desirable qualities. As Upshur *et al.* (1978) note, however, it is equally plausible that people rate as desirable the qualities they themselves possess, e.g. X is tall, therefore X considers height to be a generally desirable quality. In any case, the matrix of correlations on self-flattery that Oller quotes has something of a sting in the tail if we switch to consider social approval. One has to ask why, if approval is also of such great importance, that so many of the trait x trait correlations are so low. Surely if people are searching for the socially desirable response, there should be *uniformly* higher correlations throughout the matrix?

Generally, though, it is fruitless to pick over the data quoted by Oller. In the main he has used unvalidated measures himself, and frequently argued from the individual item level. It is more instructive to consider some of the arguments Gardner has marshalled in his own defence, and to examine the procedures he has followed in test construction. Gardner (1980) has reported research bearing on the predictive, content and construct validity of the AMI. The predictive validity argument is simply that there are substantial correlations with other variables (cf. the median correlation of 0.37, reported earlier). For content validity Gardner (1980) draws attention to the procedures of test construction that he has followed: (i) careful definition of the variables of interest, based on theory and research, (ii) generation of a pool of possible items, (iii) pre-testing to eliminate poor items. In this way he has ensured that the scales produced are reliable and homogeneous. (This contrasts sharply with most of the measures which Oller has used, which have often been single items. It is inevitable that research designs with lots of items examined singly will throw up anomalous results, which can permit many interpretations, as Gardner *et al.* (1982) demonstrates. That is why the safeguards of scale construction and the piloting and validation of measures by recycling are so important.) Further support for the validity of the AMI is provided in Gardner *et al.* (1985), a multitrait–multimethod study which demonstrates that it is the traits concerned which are primary, and that they are not at all swamped by method effects. In other words, convergent and discriminant validity were demonstrated.

Construct validity, too, has been well established. Correlational and factor analyses with the AMI and other measures have shown acceptable internal relations (e.g. Gardner and Smythe 1981, p.521) and factor structure (*op. cit.*, pp.516–17). The same applies to the data reported earlier on correlations and factor analyses with aptitude and achievement measures. The research with classroom behaviour, perseverance intentions, and acquisitional processes are similarly supportive. Finally, discriminant validity of the constructs has been established through studies which show a selective relationship between the AMI and foreign language achievement but *not* with grades in other courses (Gardner *et al.* 1979: cited in Gardner and Gliksman 1982). Other studies have shown, through factor analyses, the independence of AMI constructs from areas such as humanitarianism, and, through correlations (Gardner *et al.* 1985), from *social desirability*. There may still be some way to go in the development of reliable and valid measures of attitudes and motivation, but Gardner's work has surely demonstrated that considerable progress has already been made. The painstaking nature of the approach to scale construction should be an example to other investigators of how measurement problems can be made more tractable in the social sciences.

Motivation: cause or effect

At the beginning of the chapter it was proposed that one possible influence on motivation might be success itself, with motivation as the result, rather than the cause of achievement. In support of the 'caused' interpretation Burstall (1975) reports research with a sample of primary school children learning French. She (Burstall *et al.* 1974) took the correlations of first-year achievement measures with second-year attitude scores from which first-year attitude scores had been partialled out, and the correlations of first-year attitude scores with second-year achievement (from which first-year achievement had been partialled out). The first type of correlation turned out to be higher than the second, leading Burstall (1975) to the conclusion that it is achievement which is primary, and motivation the consequence. Hermann (1980) also argues for what she calls the resultative hypothesis. She investigated two groups of German learners of English, one group from the fifth year of instruction, the others beginners. The fifth-year group had more positive attitudes towards the target language community than the beginners, leading Hermann to conclude that instruction itself had brought about this change. The higher-proficiency learners showed no consistent pattern of integrative orientation while the less proficient students exhibited less positive attitudes and more prejudice. Hermann (1980) argued that it was the degree of success within the instruction which had produced the different motivational orientations. Strong (1984), working with 13 non-English speaking Spanish kindergarteners in a bilingual classroom, looked at the relationship between English language proficiency and the tendency to nominate and interact with English-speaking children in the classroom. He reasoned that the children who nominated English speakers as the ones they interacted with would be, by so doing, showing their integrative orientation and should, for the motivation-as-cause hypothesis to be supported, show higher proficiency. In fact the relationship obtained was non-significant, casting doubt on the original hypothesis. Strong (1984) also compared the interaction-indices of the 13 NES children with six children whose English proficiency was greater on entry to the class. He found that the initially proficient children did nominate and interact with the native English speakers in the classroom to a greater extent, leading him to the conclusion that it was the initial proficiency which had led to the greater degree of interaction with the native English speakers, and, in his terms, greater integrative orientation. Finally, Savignon (1972) is also widely quoted as supporting a resultative hypothesis, since she has published correlations between measures of the Desire to Learn French and achievement which increased in magnitude as the learner's course of study progressed.

There is, however, research support *for* the motivation-as-cause position. Gardner (1985, pp.93–8) presents data on measures of integrativeness, motivation, and attitudes towards the learning situation as a function of two variables: year of study (year 1 vs. year 2) and achievement (high vs. low). He reasons that if motivation is caused, then the measures concerned should show a strong influence for the high achievement group in the second year, i.e. by the end of the second year the *high* achievers should have developed more positive attitudes. In statistical terms one would be looking for an interaction between year of study and proficiency. On the basis of the large amount of data he collected Gardner (1985, Ch. 5) concluded that there is no real evidence of any such interaction, and that there is no evidence that differential success influences attitudes and motivation. A second line of argument against the resultative hypothesis comes from Table 4.2 above, giving the correlations between aptitude and the AMI as a function of different grade levels. Since aptitude is such a demonstrated correlate of achievement one would expect that by Grade 11 the higher aptitude students would have experienced cumulatively greater success, so one would expect the aptitude–AMI correlation to rise as a function of grade, as aptitude-mediated achievement leads to changes in motivational levels for the higher achieving students. In fact the aptitude–AMI correlations show no such trend. We might also expect the aptitude–motivation correlations to be higher when the aptitude–achievement correlations are higher. Again, they are not. So once again, the evidence does not support the resultative hypothesis.

We now have the classical problem of discrepant evidence making judgement difficult. Clearly, more research is needed, but for the moment we can scrutinize the existing results for the adequacy of the research designs that were used. For example, Gardner (1985) has attacked the partial correlation technique used by Burstall, providing statistical reasons why this should be a technique of last resort as it requires assumptions which are difficult to meet. Similarly, the Hermann (1980) study has three main shortcomings. First, no data are reported, so it is difficult for the reader to draw any independent conclusions. Second, there was no control group. It is possible that attitudes polarize anyway between the ages of 10–12 and 14–16. It is also possible that there is a relationship between attitudes and general school attainment, such that by 14–16, low achievers in all subjects, including, but not especially, languages, have less favourable attitudes to outgroups. Finally, the results for high and low achievers are not symmetrical. The low achievers are reported as being more prejudiced against the English while the high achievers did not have any consistently superior attitude or motivational orientation. If the resultative hypothesis is followed, it seems hard to explain why failure affects motivation clearly, while success does not.

One can also criticize the Strong (1984) study. First, there is the issue of generalizability. It is difficult to know what significance the integrative orientations of five- and six-year-olds have, assuming they possess any, for the importance of the construct more generally. Second, it is not completely clear how justifiable it is to regard sociometric data on the native English speaking children who were nominated as friends and interlocutors by the L1 Spanish children as relating to the construct integrative orientation. One wonders what chance factors, especially personality and teacher intervention, influence friendship patterns irrespective of any wider orientations towards language learning. Finally, the Savignon (1972) study is not as clear cut as one would like either. Using three groups with Ns of, respectively 12, 15 and 15 subjects, and 34 different variables, she calculated very large numbers of correlation coefficients. She used six criterion measures. For *one* of these only (Desire to Learn French) there was a systematic increase, longitudinally, in the correlational level between the attitude scale and achievement. For the other five achievement measures there was no such relationship. As Savignon (1972) warns, large correlational matrices (especially with such small Ns) should be interpreted with caution, since chance results confuse the overall picture. Her results cannot, therefore, be considered to be strong evidence for the resultative hypothesis.

One can similarly critique the studies in support of motivation-as-a-cause. Gardner (1985), for example, in his research looking for an interaction between year of study and proficiency, divided this latter variable into high and low groups on the basis of a median split. One wonders if interactions might have been more readily detectable if another basis for group selection had been used, perhaps based on groups more widely divergent in achievement. After all, with a median split, students differing in achievement by just one mark could be assigned to different groups. It is for this reason that McLaughlin (1980) advocates generalized regression analysis in such cases. The other evidence for a causal view of motivation, i.e. the interpretation of AMI x MLAT correlations, can also be criticized for its indirectness and the amount of inferencing that is required.

In conclusion, then, it would seem to the present writer that the quality of research evidence is slightly in support of the causal interpretation of motivation. The best-conceived study of the ones reviewed is that of Gardner (1985) despite its median split basis for group assignment. It seems that at least some of the time motivation has an independent causative role. But what is needed is more evidence which bears directly on this issue, and in which the investigator does not have to make dangerous inferences. This implies, above all, a move towards longitudinal and ethnographic methods in which the progress of a single group of learners is monitored closely over time.

Alternative motivational orientations

Gardner's (1979, 1985) work has focused mainly upon integrative and instrumental orientations, particularly the former. It is possible, as Gardner (1985, p.52) indicates, that there are other orientations. This has been investigated by Clement and Kruidenier (1983). These researchers used more diverse subjects, varying the target language being learned (English or French vs. Spanish); the ethnic group doing the learning (English vs. French Canadians); and the social milieu (unicultural English in Ontario, or French in Quebec vs. multicultural English or French in bilingual Ottawa), so generating eight subject groups. Clement and Kruidenier (1983) provided their learners with 37 reasons for learning the target language, and then factor analysed the ratings of the different reasons. The research design produced four common factors across the eight subject groups and these factors were interpreted as differing orientations for language study. Interestingly, although one of the factors was labelled instrumental, an integrative factor did not emerge. The additional three factors which were common to all groups were for friendship (the closest to an integrative orientation), travel, and knowledge or understanding. Additional factors emerged for one or two of the subject groups such as Familiarity/Involvement, and Curricular Language Importance. So we see that even a slight extension of the situation investigated was enough to enable researchers to tease out additional orientations for language study, and to demonstrate that the integrative orientation did not have as much unity as in Gardner's work.

Orientations and the nature of the cultural setting:

Gardner's earlier work (Gardner and Lambert 1959, 1972) found a more important integrative orientation factor in bilingual, bicultural Montreal than in more unicultural settings like Maine and Connecticut. In the Philippines, *instrumental* motivation was more prominent, a finding consistent with Lukmani's (1972) research in India. The more recent research by Gardner (e.g. 1980), mainly with secondary school children in Ontario, has, through the AMI, produced consistent correlations with proficiency, even though the setting is unicultural. However, it seems to be the Motivation cluster of scales from the AMI (not Integrativeness or Attitudes towards Learning) which produces the highest correlations of all (Gardner and Smythe 1981). Even more confusingly, several studies by Oller and his associates have reported negative relationships between integrativeness measures and proficiency. Oller, Hudson and Liu (1977) report a negative correlation between Chinese university students' desire to stay in the US and their English proficiency. Chihara and Oller (1978) report a negative association between Japanese students' proficiency in English and their ratings of English speakers as confident and modest. Oller, Baca and Vigil (1977) report a negative relationship between English proficiency and ratings of Anglos for a group of Mexican-American women.

These conflicting results raise the possibility that Gardner's socioeducational model generalizes with difficulty to other situations. Consequently, Clement (1980) has developed a model which is wider than that of Gardner, and which tries to account for motivation in the individual but in clear relationship to the social setting. Clement (1980) distinguishes between primary and secondary motivational processes. The former are based on attitudes of the learner towards the target language community, and, more specifically, concern the balance between the two opposing forces of integrativeness (as in Gardner's theorizing) and fear of assimilation. Greater integrativeness than fear of assimilation will lead to a positive disposition towards language learning , and vice versa. Very importantly, the way in which the result of the primary process influences learning is mediated by whether the learning situation is uni- or multicultural. In unicultural situations the primary process (integrativeness minus fear of assimilation) translates fairly directly to determine motivational levels (cf. Gardner's later research). However, in multicultural situations the primary process is mediated by the frequency and the quality of the contact that the learner has with the target language community. This, in turn, determines the learner's self-confidence and anxiety for language learning and it is this which finally accounts for motivational levels.

The Clement model raises the possibility that type of orientation may be a function of type of setting. To investigate this, Kruidenier and Clement (1986) conducted research with carefully selected sub-groups of learners to enable interesting comparisons to be made. Their research design (cf. the last section), contained two ethnolinguistic groups (anglophone vs. francophone) target languages of different socio-political status (official French or English vs. minority Spanish); and different cultural settings (unicultural vs. multicultural). Their results indicated that a friendship orientation had a greater influence upon the motivation levels of francophones, while the anglophone students' motivation was more influenced by a knowledge orientation. The travel orientation tended to be more important for those students who were learning a minority language e.g. Spanish, while learners of languages with official status in the community, i.e. French or English, were influenced by an *instrumental* orientation (cf. some of the discrepant results covered earlier, e.g. Gardner's Philippines study, and Lukmani (1972), which are more satisfactorily accounted for by Clement's model).

So we see that there is value in widening the social situation in which the role of motivation for language learning is studied. The problem now is that if the relatively limited amount of movement in existing research (e.g. from one Canadian province to another) has produced such changes in perspective, how are we to deal with other dimensions which would be revealed by even more different social situations? One could research with other minority groups in other countries, some indigenous, some immigrant, some who retain ethnolinguistic vitality and others not. One could also look at refugee groups, comparing those intending to stay in the host country as well as others intending to move on. One could examine situations which are more polarized politically, e.g. Belgium. And one could look at transient student groups, as Oller has done. Until more such research is completed, and with motivational measures as carefully constructed as those used by Gardner, we are unlikely to know how generalizable specific models of motivation are, and how close we are to a theory of language learning *situations*. At present motivational theories seem rather fragile, and, like some wines, do not travel well.

The linkage between milieu, orientation, and achievement

This is the area to which the bulk of the Gardner research has been directed in recent years, especially through the use of LISREL. However, Kruidenier and Clement's research (1986) has also used LISREL to test the Clement model. It accounts for the data analysed, suggesting that the social milieu base is not as directly connected to differing orientations as the Gardner model assumes. In fact, there is a more general point here. It is that much of the causal modelling research in motivation has been directed to finding evidence consistent with the particular model being tested. What is missing, however, is an investigation of whether other models could also account for the data, and even do it better, In Gardner's work, for example, what if MOT were changed in status to make it an exogenous variable at a similar level to INT and ALS? Or what if INT and ALS were combined? Or MOT and ALS reversed? Exploring alternative hypotheses such as these would considerably increase the value of model-testing research, and enable faster progress to be made. More generally, we need more research in varied situations to provide data which will test the various models of motivation in more searching ways. Then, by a process of eliminating the unsatisfactory theories, we are likely to attain a more comprehensive and satisfactory account of the role of motivation in language learning.

An evaluation of the role of motivation

This chapter has covered a 'layman's' analysis of motivation; general psychological theorizing; and, in most depth, theories and evidence relevant to a *specific* motivation for FL study. The 'layman's' analysis suggested four main sources for motivation – the materials/teaching used; the constraints and rewards involved; the amount of success achieved; and the goals of the student. These were arranged in a two-by-two matrix, in Figure 4.1. Materials/Teaching (the 'Intrinsic' hypothesis) and Constraints/Rewards (the 'Carrot and Stick' hypothesis) are clearly outside the learner. In other words, they are potentially capable of external manipulation, and not the *source* of IDs as they have been conceived here. The situation with Success (the Resultative hypothesis) is a little more complicated, since it may be the result of several factors. One such might be learner characteristics such as language aptitude. A second could be better teaching, with excellence of instruction leading to higher achievement for everyone. In each case, however success is achieved, it would be success itself which influenced motivation, and caused motivation to change. Finally, there is the goals cell of the matrix, which implies that influences external to the learning situation produce stable and persistent goals in the learner which, in turn, strongly influence motivational patterns. Here we would be dealing with a classic ID situation, and a motivation-as-cause interpretation.

The matrix showed, then, that there are other potential influences on motivation than individual differences in goals and orientations. The main part of this chapter has rather 'assumed out' these other influences (with the exception of the discussion of the resultative hypothesis) and focused upon the goals and belief structure of the individual to try to account for success in terms of relatively stable, internal characteristics. It is important now to broaden the discussion. Since *all* the possible determinants of motivation are plausible the goal should be not to ignore any of the motivational sources but to assess their *relative* impact. Further, there may be value in relating the impact of any one of them to other features of the educational situation as well as the social context of learning. We have reviewed evidence on the role of success (where it was claimed that, although the evidence is contradictory and far from conclusive, there is still a reasonable case that motivational levels are surprisingly independent of success), and on the different types of learner goals (where a range of research studies with positive results (e.g. Gardner 1985, Clement and Kruidenier 1986 have been reported). The main problem is that there has been virtually no research on the effects of excellence of materials or constraints/rewards on motivational levels, and this seriously limits our understanding of the functioning of motivation. Such research is urgently required.

Perhaps there should also be slightly different emphases in the *type* of research conducted. Most of the work that has been done has focused directly on IDs through scale development and multivariate statistics. Unfortunately, this is a methodology that is ill-equipped to handle external sources of influence. For that, i.e. to investigate the roles of materials, rewards, and even success, experimental manipulation, and ANOVA designs (such as Gardner's (1985) work on the resultative hypothesis) seem indicated. These would require investigators to control and manipulate relevant experimental conditions, focusing studies on specific postulated causes. The experimental approach would, that is, provide more direct evidence about the important sets of variables. An equally important research design issue concerns the need for longitudinal studies. In many cases, given the cumulative nature of learning, it might be hypothesized that various influences are multiplicative in their effects. This, essentially, is the claim that is made for integrative motivation – because it is rooted in the personality it will sustain motivation more dependably, and not be so susceptible to external changes of learning conditions, e.g. a new textbook. Similarly, with the issue of assessing causality, it seems essential to run studies which monitor motivational levels over time in some detail, rather than take the 'snapshot' approach through test administration at the beginning and end of courses. Such monitoring may be revealing about the causation of motivation at the micro level, and not force us to make assumptions about the events which have led from one beginning state to another end state. Above all, there may be a clear role for more ethnographic and observationally oriented studies of motivation which do not have the same distancing effects of other methodologies. It is to be hoped that such approaches would complement and illuminate the results from these other research traditions.

5

Language learning strategies

Introduction

The present chapter will look at language learning strategies, something of a contrast with the preceding two, since here we have the possibility of the learner exerting control over the learning process. We are concerned, that is, with choices that the learner makes, and with the possibility that the efficiency with which the learner's capacities are used can be changed. The chapter will start by simply describing various of the research studies which have been conducted. The studies will be described roughly chronologically, and fall into two groups. The first set (Fillmore, Naiman *et al.*, Rubin) were mainly carried out in the 1970s, and are more exploratory in nature. The second set (O'Malley *et al.*, Politzer and McGroarty, etc.) have been carried out in the 1980s, and have built on their predecessors to develop less observation-based instruments.

Earlier research

The Wong-Fillmore study

Lily Wong-Fillmore (1976, 1979) studied five Mexican children who were attending (English-speaking) school in California, ranging in age from 5.7 to 7.3 years. The purpose of the study was to investigate how the children increased in communicative competence in English. Each child was paired with a native American child, and their interactions were recorded for an hour each week while they were in a school playroom. Initially, it was thought that there would not be very much variation in English proficiency over the nine-month study. In fact, extremely wide differences developed, and the central problem became how to account for them. Wong-Fillmore discounted aptitude as a basis

Table 5.1:   Children's language learning strategies

Social strategies	Cognitive strategies
S-1 Join a group and act as if you understand what's going on, even if you don't. S-2 Give the impression, with a few well-chosen words, that you speak the language S-3 Count on your friends for help	C-1 Assume what people are saying is relevant to the situation at hand Metastrategy: Guess. C-2 Get some expressions you understand, and start talking C-3 Look for recurring parts in the formulas you know C-4 Make the most of what you've got C-5 Work on the big things first: save the details for later

for the variation (although this construct was not measured in any formal sense). Instead she focused on the *cognitive and social strategies* employed by the children which helped in language learning. She identified three social strategies, and five cognitive ones, as shown in Table 5.1.

Wong-Fillmore proposes that it is the three *social* strategies that are more important. The children were more interested in establishing social relationships than in learning language, but in order to establish such relations they had to learn English. The first social strategy, then, suggests that learners should join groups, and act as if they understand what's going on in them. As Wong-Fillmore says (1979, pp 209–10):

> The crucial factor was this: Because the friends believed that the learners could understand them and that communication between them was possible, they included them in activities and conversations, and this allowed the learners to assume roles in social situations and activities that made sense to them, and gave them an opportunity to observe and acquire the kind of language children use in these activities, despite their initial inability to speak or understand the language.

Wong-Fillmore matches this social strategy with the cognitive strategy of assuming that current speech is relevant to the current situation. The repetition that is built in to the utterances that surround the children, from teachers and other children alike, increases the probability that, providing that learners see the context-utterance link, learning will be rapid, since guessing will be operating in ideal circumstances.

The next social strategy is to give the impression that you can speak the language. If the first social strategy is the entree to a group, this next strategy is the justification for staying there. The second social strategy, in turn, is linked to the cognitive strategy of 'Get some expressions you understand, and start talking', since it is these expressions which are needed to put the social strategies into operation. Examples of such expressions that Wong-Fillmore gives are:

Let's go	I'm gonna tell on you
I don't care	Knock it off
I dunno	I tell you what to do
You know what?	Shaddup your mouth
I get 2 turns	Beat it
Whose turn is it?	You have to do it this way

These are clearly expressions which require relatively little detailed understanding to have taken place but which can act as the passport to group membership, particularly when one remembers that five-year-olds do not engage in the adult norm of turn-and-turn-about discourse (Cathcart 1986).

The next cognitive strategy is to look for recurring parts in the formulas, such as the expressions shown above, since such a process will be the basis for rule learning and inferring. Wong-Fillmore gives the example of the phrase 'How do you do dese?' which is progressively and slowly broken down into constituent parts which can then be used generatively. She describes the strategy as 'speak now, learn later'. Her fourth cognitive strategy is to 'make the most of what you've got'. She gives the following example:

Nora:	Anyway I making a fitching.
Observer:	A what?
Nora:	Anyway a fitching.
Observer:	Are you?
Nora:	(Looking over at Heidi's flower) Yeah, I making a flower.
Heidi:	I'm making a flower power.
Nora:	How do you make a flower power?
Heidi:	(Looks at Nora's picture which is clearly a fish) That's not a flower.
Nora:	Yeah it is.
Heidi:	What is that anyway?
Nora:	Anyway a flower. That what is that anyway.

In the transcript, Nora uses 'anyway' just about anywhere she can. Although overdoing things, Nora manages to keep the conversation going, is able to give it a semblance of fluency, all the while pushing herself to learn how to use the term appropriately.

The final cognitive strategy is 'Work on the big things first, save the details for later'. This implies that children who focus on details are likely not be able to assemble these details in a larger system, while children who go for a larger scale of operation will be drawn, over time, into the detail they need. Wong-Fillmore's final social strategy is 'Count on your friends for help'. Some learners, that is, were more confident that native speaking partners would accept them and help them in the interaction. And because native speaking children believed that the learners could learn, these friends talked, and interacted with them in ways that guaranteed that they would.

The 'good language learner' research

Building upon introspective work by Stern (1975) a group of Canadian researchers (Naiman, Frohlich, Todesco and Stern 1978) planned to interview a sample of successful and unsuccessful language learners to gather information about the strategies they had used while learning languages. Despite these original aims, Naiman *et al.* (1978) eventually restricted their study to *good* language learners (GLLs): they were not really able to interview a wide range of unsuccessful learners. Consequently, the results they obtained will have to be treated with a little caution because there is always the possibility that the 'good' learning strategies they uncovered are also used by *bad* language learners, but other reasons cause them to be unsuccessful with this group, i.e. the GLL strategies cannot be claimed to be causal.

On the basis of 34 interviews with successful language learners a set of five major strategies were identified. In addition, each major strategy is associated with a number of minor and more specific sub-strategies. Here are the strategies, followed by example minor strategies:

Strategy 1: ACTIVE TASK APPROACH: *Good language learners actively involve themselves in the language learning task.*

(a) by responding positively to the given learning opportunities, or by identifying and seeking preferred learning environments and exploiting them.
(b) by adding related language learning activities to the regular programme, and/or intensifying their efforts.
(c) by engaging in a number of practice activities
(d) by changing the purpose of an activity in order to focus on L2 learning.

Strategy 2: REALIZATION OF LANGUAGE AS A SYSTEM: *Good language learners develop or exploit an awareness of language as a system. In dealing with language as a system, GLLs*

(a) refer back to their native language judiciously (translate into L1) and make effective cross-lingual comparisons at different stages of language learning.

(b) analyse the target language and make inferences about it.

Strategy 3: REALIZATION OF LANGUAGE AS A MEANS OF COMMUNICATION AND INTERACTION: *GLLS develop and exploit an awareness of language as a means of communication (i.e. conveying and receiving messages) and interaction (i.e. behaving in a culturally appropriate manner).*

(a) In the earlier stages of language learning GLLs may emphasize fluency over accuracy.

(b) GLLs seek out situations in which they can communicate with members of the target language and/or increase their communicative skills in the language.

(c) GLLs display critical sensitivity to language use, for example, by attempting to find out socio-cultural meanings.

Strategy 4: MANAGEMENT OF AFFECTIVE DEMANDS: *GLLs realize initially or with time that they must cope with affective demands made upon them by language learning and succeed in doing so.*

Strategy 5: MONITORING OF L2 PERFORMANCE: *GLLs constantly revise their L2 systems. They monitor the language they are acquiring by testing their inferences (guesses): by looking for needed adjustments as they learn new material or by asking native informants when they think corrections are needed.*

In addition to this list of strategies, Naiman *et al*. (1978) uncovered a large number of much more specific *techniques*. Some of the most commonly used were:

- repeating aloud after the teacher and/or native speaker (mentioned by 16 out of 34 learners)
- following the rules as given by the grammar books or textbooks (12)
- making up vocabulary charts and memorizing them (14)
- listening to radio, TV, records, etc. (21)
- having contact with native speakers (23)
- reading anything: magazines, newspapers, professional articles, comics (18)

The GLL study demonstrates the richness that can come from biographical, semi-structured data elicitation, since it achieves much greater levels of detail than the strategies originally proposed by Stern (1975) on the basis of introspective evidence.

The work of Joan Rubin

Rubin (1981) reported on conventional language learning settings with young adult learners and concentrated on the cognitive processes they used. Initially, a classroom observation schedule was used to gather data, but this approach did not yield useful results. Classrooms emphasized accuracy and teacher control rather than learning processes, and the fast-moving nature of classroom work made access to students' thoughts impossible. Some improvement resulted in researching with specific (rather than general) classroom activities, but this had the disadvantage that the strategies observed were rather task-specific, e.g. knowledge of narrative structure in a strip-story-telling task. Rubin also used an unstructured self-report technique, but this too did not produce encouraging results. Reports were often vague and not informative. Very interestingly, though, there were certainly IDs in relation to the capacity to *report* strategies – some students seemed far more able to do this than others.

The final technique used by Rubin was *directed* self-report, with a focus on particular types of cognitive process, rather than the whole range. This certainly proved to be the most successful method, and allowed Rubin to propose the following list of strategies:

1 *Clarification/verification*
   e.g. (a) Asks for example of how to use a word/expression
       (b) Puts word in sentence to check understanding
       (c) Looks up word in the dictionary
       (d) Paraphrases a sentence to check understanding.

2 *Monitoring*
   e.g. (a) Corrects error in own/other's pronunciation, vocabulary, spelling, grammar, style.
       (b) Notes sources of own errors, e.g. own language interference, other language interference.

3 *Memorization*
   e.g. (a) Takes notes of new items with or without examples, contexts, or definitions.
       (b) Finds some association (semantic, visual, etc.)

4 *Guessing/Inductive inferencing*
   e.g. (a) Uses clues from the following to guess the meaning
           – other items in the sentence or phrase
           – syntactic structure
           – context of discourse, etc., etc.
       (b) Ignores difficult word order

5 *Deductive reasoning*: Looks for and uses general rules
   e.g. (a) Compares native/other language to target language to identify similarities and differences
       (b) Infers grammatical rules by analogy

    (c) Notes exceptions to rules
    (d) Finds meaning by breaking down word into parts

6 *Practice*
    e.g. (a) Experiments with new sounds in isolation and in context, uses mirror for practice
        (b) Talks to self in target language
        (c) Drills self on words in different forms

The strategies all have a cognitive orientation, and suggest considerable scope for self-awareness in the process of learning. In this respect, one can distinguish between the strategies which emphasize on-the-spot learning ('direct' strategies, in Rubin's terms) such as clarification/verification, guessing/inductive inferencing, and deductive reasoning, and those other strategies which emphasize out-of-class activities ('indirect' strategies (Rubin 1981)), i.e. monitoring, memorization, and practice.

A comparison and evaluation of the earlier strategy research

This earlier research is very rich in findings, and also very exploratory. For that reason the following sections will examine some of the factors which have emerged as important, i.e. data elicitation techniques; subject selection; and the use of self-report data. It will then survey and collate the findings from the different studies and offer some interim conclusions.

Data elicitation
The research by Wong-Fillmore (1976) and Naiman *et al*. (1978) is very much in the research-then-theory perspective (cf. discussion in Chapter 1, and in McLaughlin 1987). In Wong-Fillmore's case, ethnographic/observational methods were used in fairly natural settings, while with Naiman *et al*. the respondents in the semi-structured interview were given considerable freedom to cover any material that they thought relevant. In each case the investigator was meant to have few preconceptions, and it was the respondents who were to be directive. Rubin's data elicitation procedure was much more structured. She was guided by a set of hypotheses loosely relating cognitive functioning to language acquisition. These could not be really characterized as a theory so much as a set of working assumptions, i.e. bases for research which looked for the instantiation of pre-existing categories.

Subject selection
The studies also differ from one another in their selection of subjects. Wong-Fillmore worked with only five, all young children. We do not

know how typical they were of the relevant population of five-year-olds, let alone children of different ethnic backgrounds or ages. The detail of the ethnographic work and the greater confidence that comes with it necessarily requires compromise in terms of generality and representativeness (Long 1983a). Rubin's research mostly used young adults as subjects, e.g. students who happened to be taking ESL classes at the University of Hawaii, mainly of Japanese background, or applied linguistics students who, essentially, kept diaries of their language learning. In contrast, Naiman *et al.* (1978) based their study on *successful* (and often *extremely* successful) language learners who were identified through colleagues from the university environment. Most of these were highly educated people, and it could not be claimed (nor was it) that these subjects were representative of the general population.

Self-report data

Seliger (1983) argues that any self-report data, since they cannot be independently confirmed, should be treated with caution. Retrospection, for example, might well mean favourable re-editing by the learner, or perhaps, recreation of what might reasonably have happened so that the data-gatherer can be humoured with some data to take away! It is also possible that the act of reporting data may interfere with it, a claim rejected by Cohen (1983). There is an even greater complication. This is that what accounts for the reporting of the strategies *and* the language learning success are the same thing – greater powers of articulateness. It is possible, in other words, that some people are capable of more precise, detailed and organized thought perhaps because of decontextualization ability, analytic capacities with verbal material, or memory, or other factors. This is what enables them to reflect on their own language learning experiences effectively, and report them so well. *These same abilities may be those which are also important in language learning success.* Less successful learners may not have experienced success for the same reason they could not report strategies, i.e. lack of these very same capacities. Consequently, retrospective accounts in such cases may not enable us to identify what the causal variables are, and to choose between the two competing 'explanations' given above. Results from such studies, interesting as they are, would be important input for the framing of hypotheses (Seliger 1983) which would need to be tested by setting up effective conditions to allow researchers to tease apart whether the strategies themselves or the articulateness which might underlie them are the causal variables. One would need, that is, a more controlled, experimental approach at a second stage of research.

Findings

The final area for comparison between these early studies concerns the actual findings. The main strategies identified by the different inves-

Table 5.2: Comparison of findings from earlier strategy research

Naiman *et al.*	Rubin	Wong-Fillmore Social	Cognitive
1 Active task approach	1 Clarification verification	1 Join a group	1 Assume relevance of what is being said
2 Language is a system	2 Memorization	2 Give the impression you can speak the language	2 Get some expressions
3 Language is a means of communication and interaction	3 Guessing, inductive inferencing	3 Count on your friends	3 Look for recurring parts in formulae
4 Management of affective demands	4 Deductive reasoning		4 Make the most of what of what you've got
5 Monitoring of performance	5 Monitoring		5 Work on the big things first

tigators are presented together, in abbreviated form, in Table 5.2.

The table reveals interesting similarities and differences between the investigators. For example, Naiman *et al.* (1978) give their primary strategy as that of using an *Active Task Approach*. This would seem to embrace Rubin's 'clarification/verification', 'memorization', and 'practice' strategies, on the one hand, and Wong-Fillmore's 'get some expressions' and 'make the most of what you've got'. It is also the superordinate category for all Wong-Fillmore's Social Strategies. In a similar way, Naiman *et al.*'s second strategy, *Realization of Language as a System*, seems to contain Rubin's 'guessing/inductive inferencing' and 'deductive reasoning', as well, perhaps, as Wong-Fillmore's 'look for recurring parts in formulae'. Finally, Naiman *et al.*'s *Monitoring of Performance* strategy has its counterpart in Rubin's 'monitoring'. So, to sum up, the similarities concern the learner's capacity to impose himself on the learning situation; his technical predispositions; and his capacity to evaluate.

The first sorts of differences that emerge are those where strategies proposed by one researcher are not matched by the others. Naiman *et al.*'s (1978) *Management of Affective Demands* clearly comes into this category, as does Wong-Fillmore's *Work On The Big Things First*. Beyond this fairly obvious level of difference, there are others which are, perhaps, more significant. Above all, Naiman and Rubin, since they are dealing with adults, take account of the *reflections of learners about their own learning*. For example, the Monitoring strategy implies a capacity to relate one's progress to an evaluative framework, and to distance oneself from the actual learning, abilities beyond Wong-Fillmore's young learners. In addition, consciousness of learning is also important with the *Realization of Language as a System* strategy. Naiman *et al.* (1978) mention referring back to the L1, and to the use of inferencing; and Rubin similarly includes guessing and inferencing as well as deductive reasoning. Naiman and Rubin seem, therefore, to assume quite powerful metacognitive abilities while Wong-Fillmore is more concerned with immediate, context-dependent language use. Related to this, Naiman and Rubin, on the one hand, and Wong-Fillmore, on the other, also differ in terms of the situations in which relevant activity occurs. For Wong-Fillmore this is almost exclusively during actual language functioning – learning to talk involves talking to learn. This too is important for the other researchers, but Naiman and Rubin extend their analysis to include situations where language *use* is not involved, but where relevant activity is. Each of them, for example, mentions practice and memorization as important activities.

There are also important differences regarding the language learning theories that are implicit in the work of each investigator. Wong-Fillmore sees progress as being a slow, hard-won process in which the development of the language *system* arises slowly, almost grudgingly, out of the use of formulaic speech. In addition, Wong-Fillmore's 'theory' of language learning stresses that the context of speech is important for guessing meaning (C1: Assume relevance). There is, therefore, a strong comprehension-driven element to most effective progress, with the environment providing the clues *for those children most willing and able to exploit them* to enable language to be understood. In contrast, the work by Naiman *et al.* (1978) and Rubin (1981) emphasizes the development of a *system through analysis*. Rubin covers two major processes: guessing/inductive inferencing and deductive reasoning, implying a learner for whom mental processing and mental transformation, not necessarily linguistic, are pre-eminent. Naiman *et al.* (1978) also emphasize analysis, and, although they are less precise, they do indicate that linguistic material is involved, e.g. 'refer back to the L1 judiciously'. They emphasize the benefits of perceiving the systematic nature of language, while Rubin focuses more on general processes of cognition.

Finally, there is the issue of the amount of time spent learning. Some behaviours, e.g. deductive reasoning, contribute fairly directly to the *process* of language learning. In contrast, Naiman's *Active Task Approach*, Wong-Fillmore's *Social Strategies*. Rubin's *Memorization* and *Practice* all have the effect that more time is actually spent learning.

This may be important in predicting success but it is also disappointing as an explanatory account, since time is a fairly unilluminating causal agent. What would be more interesting would be the identification of strategies which can selectively improve the *efficiency* of instruction and therefore hold out the prospect of successful *intervention*, rather than simply reflecting more application.

Interim conclusions
If then we look at the range of studies, we are left with something of a conundrum. The studies covered have not been of an experimental nature, and as such have not established *causes* of success. Where strategies involve self-report, it is logically possible that the success associated with learning strategies *as well as the strategies themselves* are both due to a further underlying cause – the ability to analyse, to reflect, to be more precise in one's thoughts as well as to be articulate about them. Further, all the studies differ from one another methodologically. Still, as an interim assessment, four generalizations can be proposed:

1 Social strategies seem to be the most clearly established in importance when informal language learning is involved. They maximize exposure to the target language, and interaction opportunities.
2 A large class of strategies concern the *amount of time spent learning*, e.g. the social strategies.
3 There are different versions of learning theory underlying the different investigators' work, mainly contrasting the learning of a system with formulaic, non-analytic learning.
4 There does seem to be some agreement that reflective abilities are important in all but the younger learners.

Recent studies of learner strategies

Politzer and McGroarty

The Politzer and McGroarty study (1985) was based on a questionnaire administered to a group of 37 students preparing for postgraduate study in the United States in an intensive eight-week English course. The group was made up of approximately equal numbers of Hispanic and Asian students. In addition to the questionnaires, students were given three pre- and post-course proficiency tests: an aural comprehension test, a grammar test, and a communicative competence test. The questionnaire, the heart of the study, consisted of three sections, (i) a 14-item scale on classroom behaviours; (ii) a 15-item scale on individual study; and (iii) a 22-item scale on interaction with others outside the classroom. The sources for the items in the scales were diverse.

Table 5.3:   Items from Politzer and McGroarty's scales

Classroom behaviour

6   Do you interrupt yourself when you notice that you have made a mistake?

8* Do you speak to fellow students (in class) in your native language?

12 Do you ask the teacher *when* and *by whom* an expression can be used?

14 Do you often guess the meaning of new words from the rest of the sentence in which they are used?

Learning behaviour during individual study

3   Do you sometimes think about differences between English and your native language and – as a result – avoid making mistakes?

4* Do you try to memorize sentences as much as possible *without* analysing them by grammar rules?

11 Do you keep track (e.g. by checking vocabulary lists or vocabulary cards) of words that you have learned?

12* When memorizing words or phrases, do you generally associate them with words or phrases in your native language rather with other words or phrases in English or with pictures or actions?

Interactions with others outside the classroom

2   If you see that someone does not understand you, do you often try to rephrase what you are saying?

3   If you are not sure whether what you said is grammatically correct, do you ask for confirmation?

8   Can you often guess the meaning of what somebody said either from his/her expression or from gestures?

18* In social gatherings, do you, whenever possible, try to talk to individuals who speak your native language?

---

* = An answer of 'No' is regarded as the 'positive' strategy.

Some reflected the hypotheses of the investigators. Many of the items are operationalizations in questionnaire item form, of the insights arising from the studies of Naiman *et al.* (1978), and Rubin (1981). Some of the items from the scales will help to make this clear.

The scales were examined for internal consistency by inspection of item–total correlations and it was discovered that the scales were not very reliable. The Classroom Behaviour reliability coefficient was 0.45; Individual Study was 0.24; Interaction 0.23, all very low figures, suggesting rather unfocused scales. To improve the reliability figures, items with negative item–total correlations were eliminated. From the items shown in Table 5.3, items 6 and 8 from the Classroom scale, 4 and 12 from the Individual Study scale, and 2 and 8 from Interaction were eliminated. (In total, out of 51 items, 19 were eliminated at this stage.) These changes produced scales with much greater homogeneity, and the reliability coefficients increased to 0.52, 0.61, and 0.63, respectively. However, we are left with the problem that we have no basis, other than blind statistics, for accepting or rejecting items. Some good items, as we shall see, may have been eliminated.

Politzer and McGroarty next examined whether the *items* (not the scales) related to *gain scores* on the proficiency tests. In fact, only a few of the items did relate significantly to these scores. Four items from the Classroom scale (out of 14) entered into significant relationships; 4 (out of 15) for the Individual Study related; and 2 (out of 22) for the Inter-action scale. Even more worrying are some of the characteristics of successful items. Four of the 10 successful items were amongst those which had been 'eliminated' because they showed *negative* item–total correlations and appeared to be working in the opposite direction to the scale as a whole, i.e. from Table 5.4, items 6 (Classroom Behaviour), and 12 (Individual Study). In relation to the different criterion tests, the picture becomes even more complicated. Item 12, on L1/L2 associa-tions, related positively with the communicative competence test (i.e. L2 associations are good), and negatively with the multiple-choice grammar test (i.e. L1 associations are good!). With item 13, on extra time spent practicing, answering 'Yes' (the predicted 'good' answer) is associated with better performance on the grammar test, but *worse* per-formance on the comprehension and communicative competence tests. (Interestingly, one can quickly advance *ad hoc* explanations for these conflicting results, but these explanations would have to assume strange relationships between the criterion measures.)

Finally, Politzer and McGroarty found several interactions between learner strategies and ethnic background. The Hispanic students scored significantly higher than the Asian students on all the Learning Beha-viour scales, especially on Interaction, suggesting that the Hispanic stu-dents should be more successful language learners. However the only significant difference between the gain scores of the Hispanic students and the Asian students was on the discrete point scored form of the communicative competence test, and the greater gain was for the *Asian* students.

We need now to draw some conclusions from the Politzer and McGroarty study. Judged by results, it is clearly not very successful. The scales concerned did distinguish between the two ethnic groups but lacked internal consistency, and did not translate into meaningful results at the item level. If we think of the study as provisional, how-ever, there is a great deal to be learned. For example, in relation to ethnic background, it is clear that strategies research is culturally loaded. As Politzer and McGroarty point out, different groups may have different norms for behaviour, and we can only interpret these behaviours within the set of cultural assumptions that hold within each group. A second factor concerns the nature of the criterion test.

Politzer and McGroarty included three criterion tests, and found different relationships between them and the strategies items. This suggests that future studies will need to have differentiated measures of language proficiency to allow complexity of interrelationships to emerge.

The Politzer and McGroarty study is also instructive if we use it to consider how we would expect items to function, and what sort of answers we label 'desirable'. Question 4 from the *Individual Study* section is 'Do you memorize sentences as much as possible without analysing them through grammatical rules?. A negative response was deemed the 'good' response, thus connecting with the GLL strategy of Realization of Language as a System. However, a positive or 'bad' response might also have its attractions in terms of Wong-Fillmore's formulaic learning and strategy of 'Get some expressions . . . ' and the aptitude-based learner type who relies on memory-driven, unanalysed language. (In fact, the item had a negative correlation with the total scale, suggesting that the Wong-Fillmore/learner-type interpretation was more appropriate.) Politzer and McGroarty (1985, p.110), draw attention to some other problems with responses to questionnaire items. 'Do you often look words up in a dictionary?' could, they suggest, be associated with a bad, dictionary-dependent student, rather than an assiduous systematic one. Many of the other behaviours could be similarly interpreted, such as asking for help, using gestures), etc. As a result, questionnaire-derived information may have been extensively 'filtered' by the respondents, and what constitutes a 'good' response is by no means obvious on logical grounds. Statistical investigation has to supplement the original insights before they can be accepted.

In many ways the Politzer and McGroarty study is exemplary. It includes many crucial variables, and has a research design which lays the groundwork for many important questions to be addressed. It also seemed to be well timed to build upon the insights arising from the more biographical or observationally oriented strategies research. In the final analysis, however, it has to be judged unsuccessful. The empirical data, either in terms of internal consistency of the scales, or of their validity, is not impressive. As an exploratory study, it is interesting and provides the basis for further questionnaire-based studies, indeed it is vital that such studies are run. But for the present, such a research strategy has not yet paid dividends.

The O'Malley *et al.* research

Another major research programme in the 1980s had been that conducted by O'Malley, Chamot, Stewner-Manzares, Kupper and Russo (1985a, b) in the United States. In a first study, O'Malley *et al.* (1985a) collected strategy data on the basis of interviews with secondary-school

ESL learners, interviews with their teachers and observation. The teacher interviews and the observations did not yield very productive data, and the focus for the research became the self-report data. This was obtained by talking to the children in groups of three to five about nine specific oral language learning tasks. Seven of these tasks were drawn from typical ESL activities, i.e. pronunciation, oral drills and grammar exercises, vocabulary. The other two activities were from situations outside the classroom. Interviewers asked for strategy reports for the various activities, but could if necessary use a list of prompts based on a literature review. The 26 strategies which O'Malley *et al.* (1985a) identified are shown in Table 5.4.

It is striking that many of the strategies reported by Naiman *et al.* (1978) and Wong-Fillmore (1976, 1979) are not included here. There is little emphasis on the Strategy of Realization of Language as a Means of Communication (GLL 2), or Management of Affective Demands (GLL 4), or on Wong-Fillmore's social strategies. There is little concern, either, with the interaction and input-maximizing strategies that Naiman *et al.* (1978) and Wong-Fillmore (1976) were so concerned about. No doubt this reflects the different settings for the respective studies, i.e. classrooms vs. naturalistic environments. Even so, the difference is striking, and not compensated for by O'Malley *et al.*'s (1985a) one socially oriented strategy, cooperation, which seems to have had far less impact on learning.

But equally striking is the greater focus on metacognitive strategies, of which there are nine. These correspond slightly to the Monitoring strategies mentioned by Naiman *et al.* (1978) and Rubin (1981), but for O'Malley *et al.* (1985a) monitoring is only one amongst a number of metacognitive strategies. There is, basically, a considerably enlarged role for the learner as a self-reflective being, with insight into, and control over, his own learning processes, insights which can be harnessed to enable gains in learning efficiency. As O'Malley *et al.* (1985b) put it:

Metacognitive strategies involve thinking about the learning process, planning for learning, monitoring of comprehension or production while it is taking place, and self-evaluation of learning after the language activity is completed. Cognitive strategies are more directly related to individual learning tasks and entail direct manipulation or transformation of the learning materials. . . . *This line of research suggests that transfer of strategy training to new tasks can be maximized by pairing cognitive strategies with appropriate metacognitive strategies. Students without metacognitive approaches are essentially learners without direction or opportunity to review their progress, accomplishments, and future directions.* O'Malley *et al.* (1985b, pp.560–1: Emphasis added.)

Table 5.4:   Learning strategy definitions

LEARNING STRATEGY	DESCRIPTION
A. METACOGNITIVE STRATEGIES	
Advance organizers	Making a preview of the organizing concept or principle in a learning activity
Directed attention	Deciding in advance what to attend to in a learning task.
Selective attention	Deciding in advance to attend to specific aspects of the language input or situational details in a task.
Self-management	Understanding and arranging for the conditions that help one learn.
Advance preparation	Planning for and rehearsing linguistic components necessary for a language task.
Self-monitoring	Correcting one's speech for accuracy or for appropriateness to context.
Delayed production	Consciously deciding to postpone speaking in favour of initial listening.
Self-evaluation	Checking learning outcomes against internal standards.
Self-reinforcement	Arranging rewards for successfully completing a language learning activity.
B: COGNITIVE STRATEGIES	
Repetition	Imitating a language model, including overt practice and silent rehearsal
Resourcing	Using target language reference materials
Directed physical response	Relating new information to physical actions as with directives.
Translation	Using the first language to understand and produce the second language.
Grouping	Reordering or reclassifying material to be learned.
Note-taking	Writing down main ideas, important points, outlines, or summaries of information.
Deduction	Conscious application of rules.
Recombination	Constructing language by combining known elements in a new way
Imagery	Relating new information to visual concepts in memory.
Auditory representation	Retention of the sound or similar sound for a word, phrase, etc.
Keyword	Remembering a new word in the second language by mnemonic or associational techniques, e.g. keywords.
Contextualisation	Placing a word or phrase in a meaningful language sequence.
Elaboration	Relating new information to existing concepts

Table 5.4: *continued*

Transfer	Using previously acquired knowledge to facilitate new learning.
Inferencing	Using available information to guess meanings of new items, predict outcomes, etc.
Question for clarification	Asking a teacher, etc. for for repetition, paraphrasing, explanation, and/or examples.
C: SOCIAL MEDIATION	
Cooperation	Working with one or more peers to obtain feedback, pool information, etc.

O'Malley *et al*. (1985a) also reported results linking proficiency level to strategy use. There is a slight tendency for intermediate level students to use a greater proportion of metacognitive strategies, as though they are more aware of themselves as learners and invest greater efforts in controlling and directing what they do, whereas the beginning level learners emphasize more the actual handling of data, and direct learning processes. Even so, cognitive strategies predominate for both groups. O'Malley *et al*. (1985a, pp.38–9) give the following order of strategy use:

(a) Repetition (14.8%); Note-taking (14.1%)
(b) Clarification (12.8%); Cooperation (11.7%)
(c) Imagery (9.4%); Translation (8.5%); Transfer (7.8%); Inferencing (7.2%)
(d) Elaboration (2.5%); Key Word (0.2%); Deduction (0.4%); Grouping (0.9%); Recombination (0.4%)

The most frequently used strategies tend to be concerned with rote learning, and not transformation or engagement with the learning material, a disappointing finding in that evidence from cognitive psychology suggests that depth of processing (Craik and Lockhart 1972) is an important influence upon effective learning, as is the reorganization and transformation of material (Wickelgren 1979, Anderson 1985). This tendency is corroborated where strategy use is linked to tasks. Greater strategy use tends to be linked to activities which are less complex conceptually. The most strategy generating activities, for example, were vocabulary learning, pronunciation, and oral drills. Fewer strategies were used in more complex activities like analysis, inferencing and making oral presentations.

O'Malley *et al*. (1985b) were also interested in the trainability of strategies. A group of 75 ESL high-school students were randomly assigned to one of the three conditions. The first group, Experimental 1, were provided with strategy training on a listening task with the metacognitive strategy of selective attention (i.e. listening for specific linguistic markers), the cognitive strategy of note-taking (i.e. structured support to improve note-taking organization), and cooperation (i.e. questioning other students about gaps in notes, and pooling information). The second group, Experimental 2, received training in the cognitive and socioaffective strategies, but not the metacognitive one of selective attention. The control group simply viewed the videotapes which had been the basis for the strategy training, and were asked to do what they normally did during lecture comprehension. For speaking, students were required to present a brief oral report. The Experimental 1 group were given training in analysing the communicative requirements of the communication task, e.g. its organizational structure. For the cooperation strategy, oral reports were presented to other students and the presenting student was given guidance as to how to solicit feedback. The cognitive group students received instruction in the cooperation strategy, but not in the metacognitive strategy of functional practice. The control group were simply asked to prepare an oral report in the way they were accustomed. The various groups were given pre- and post-tests (as well as some in-course tests) to assess the effect of the strategy training. The results are shown in Table 5.5. Quite clearly there are few significant differences. The speaking test is significant beyond the 0.01 level, as is the second daily listening test. In addition, the third daily listening test is significant at the 0.05 level. The results, therefore, provide only limited supporting evidence for the effectiveness of strategy training.

It is difficult to draw conclusions from such a study since so many variables remain uninvestigated. For example, a small number of strategies (four) were arbitrarily selected out of a much larger set (of 26): we do not know whether other strategies or combinations of strategies would have been more effectively trainable. Equally important to stra-

Table 5.5: Effects of strategy training on test performance

	Metacognitive	Cognitive	Control	p
Post tests				
Listening	8.25	8.18	7.30	.162
Speaking	3.60	3.04	2.88	.008**
Daily tests of listening				
1	6.03	5.91	5.46	.096
2	6.45	6.54	5.45	.004**
3	6.27	6.95	5.17	.043*
4	5.25	5.10	5.09	.626

$* = p < .05$ $** = p < .01$

tegy selection is the issue of *timing*. The O'Malley *et al.* (1985b) research was based on an intervention period which was, by any standards, brief. Since we do not know how long it takes to train strategies, or whether different strategies require different training periods to be effective, we cannot really say whether the training procedures used by O'Malley *et al.* (1985b) were adequate. This, in turn, connects with the issue of *strategy specificity*, of the extent to which strategies transfer, and of their domains of operation. We would expect the metacognitive strategies to transfer more generally than the cognitive strategies. Because of the significant effect of a metacognitive strategy on speaking, for example (analysing communicative requirements), one would like to see that students are able to make similar analyses of comparable situations, and act upon these analyses. However, at present, we cannot rule out the possibility that no more than a performance strategy linked to a specific situation produced the significant effect. The question can only be addressed when more research accumulates which tests this issue adequately, and we have an idea of which strategies, metacognitive or otherwise, are pervasive in their effects.

A final aspect of the O'Malley *et al.* (1985a, b) research, which goes well beyond the issue of strategy trainability, is the connection that the work has with other areas. In particular, O'Malley *et al.* (1985b, Chamot and O'Malley 1987) discuss the issue of metacognitive strategies in relation to the decontextualized language of classroom performance. Learners who use such strategies would seem well adapted to what goes on in typical classrooms, since such classrooms presuppose such skills. We are back, in other words, to the discussion of decontextualized language provided in Chapter 3, where it was proposed (Skehan 1986c) that part of the reason aptitude tests predict well is that they reflect a decontextualization ability. In fact, the strategies literature, by mention of such specific areas as using advance organizers, directed and selective attention, self-management, self-monitoring, and self-evaluation, is more precise in many areas about the actual decontextualized skills that are implicated in learning. Such precision could have beneficial influence on other areas of ID research.

Other research

Huang and Van Naerssen (1985) used a research design comparing the learning strategies used by the top and bottom thirds in a group of 60 graduating students from the Guangzhou Foreign Languages Institute. They wanted to discover whether the two groups, whose composition had been determined on the basis of performance on an oral test, relied upon different language learning strategies. Strategy data were collected by means of a questionnaire on learner strategies, and an in-depth interview. The questionnaire, which was influenced by the work of Rubin (1975), Stern (1975), and Bialystok (1978, 1979), gathered data on the use of formal practice, functional practice and monitoring – three of the major influences on learning described in Bialystok's (1979) model. The questionnaire emphasized strategy use *outside* the formal classroom, i.e. opportunities for language use that the learners themselves chose.

No significant differences were found for the high vs. low proficiency groups for the use of formal practice or monitoring. There were significant differences, though (at the 0.05 level), for the use of functional practice, just as Bialystok (1978, 1979) had found, with high-proficiency students reporting greater use of these strategies. The functional strategies category was, in fact, made up of several component strategies. When these were examined separately, (i) speaking the L2 with other students, teachers, and native speakers; (ii) thinking in English; and (iii) participation in group oral communicative activities produced significant differences (all beyond the 0.01 level) between the high and low groups. The other functional practice strategy, attending lectures, and watching TV and films, did not produce a significant difference between the two groups.

These results are interpreted by Huang and Van Naerssen (1985) as indicating the usefulness of functional practice strategies, thus corroborating the research reported by Bialystok (1979) which derives from her model of language learning. There are two problems, however, which suggest that some caution is required. First, as we have mentioned, the subjects concerned were graduates of a Foreign Languages Institute. This would suggest that *all* of them must have already demonstrated considerable educational and linguistic talent to reach this position at all. Generalization to other groups is therefore hazardous, since the linguistic accomplishments of the low group might well be the envy of most people. Second, there is the issue of causality. Greater strategy use might lead some students to higher levels of performance. Equally, higher performance might enable the use of more strategies. The proficiency-causes-strategies explanation is given some limited support by two aspects of the research. Huang and Van Naerssen (1985, p.293) report that

> although certain unsuccessful students . . . attempted to adopt the . . . techniques used by their more successful peers, they found that those techniques were not very helpful in their cases.

In addition, it is striking that the one functional practice strategy which was not significant (attending lectures, etc.) is the one that least implicates proficiency to engage in strategy use. The research design cannot separate out the two possibilities of strategies-as-caused and strategies-as-causal. For that a longitudinal study and the monitoring of change over time would be necessary.

Chesterfield and Chesterfield (1985) have also researched into strategy use, but this time with young children (of 5 to 6 years of age). They studied 14 Mexican-American children in bilingual classrooms. Data collection was by means of participant observation, field notes, and subsequent codings of the strategies revealed by the children. The strategies which were studied were influenced by the work of Rubin (1981), Bialystok (1981), and Tarone (1983) (even though these investigators had mainly studied much older learners), and used categories like repetition, elaboration, requests for clarification and role play.

Several aspects of the Chesterfield *et al.* (1985) research merit comment. First of all, they successfully used observational data. In this they contrast with Rubin (1981) and O'Malley *et al.* (1985a, b) who both encountered difficulties with such an approach. One wonders whether the younger learners in the Chesterfield *et al.* (1985) study rely on strategies which are more overtly manifested, and hence are codable, while by the ages of the learners in the other studies, these strategies have been internalized, and so are not amenable to observational data collection methods.

The second important feature of the Chesterfield and Chesterfield (1985) study is the way they have studied the longitudinal development of strategies. Eight of the children were observed at three points during their first year of schooling. This allows study of (a) variation within the group of eight children at any one time, and (b) variation in each of the children separately *over* time. Chesterfield *et al.* (1985) analysed this data set by means of an implicational scaling technique (see Tarone 1988 for more extended coverage of this technique). This form of data presentation captures systematicity and variability in the data. It allows one to see whether there is a sequence in emergence for the strategies, and whether, at any one point in time, different children are simply at different points along this sequence. It is a method, that is, of relating cross-sectional and longitudinal data, and allowing inferences about change *over* time to be made on the basis of variation in performance *at* a single time.

Chesterfield *et al.* (1985) report considerable systematicity in strategy emergence amongst their subjects, supporting the proposition that, in this case, strategy difficulty at a point in time is indicative of the order of emergence of learner strategies over time. The strategies which first appear (Chesterfield *et al.* 1985, p.56) are mainly receptive and self-contained, e.g. repetition, memorization and formulaic expression. Subsequently strategies emerge which permit interaction, e.g. verbal attention getting, appeal for assistance, requests for clarification and role play, or which reflect metacognitive abilities, awareness, and a capacity to look at language as an object of study in itself, elaboration and monitoring. It is noteworthy that there is a relationship between the Chesterfield *et al.* (1985) order of emergence, and the O'Malley *et al.* (1985a) frequency of use data. There, too, strategies like memorization were very frequently used, while metacognitive abilities were more rarely observed. O'Malley *et al.* (1985a) relate their frequency ordering to a contrast between operations which deal with simple units of language directly, e.g. memorization, and other operations which transform the material being processed in some way. This contrast, direct vs. transformed/elaborated processing, seems relevant to the Chesterfields' work too.

Learner strategies: an evaluation

Learner strategy research is in its infancy, and compared to IDs such as aptitude and motivation, one would have to place strategies research even further to the end of the research-then-theory continuum. We are still fumbling to establish a satisfactory methodology for such research, and to identify satisfactory generalizations to express what has been discovered. This final section of the chapter will survey the findings in strategies research, and then examine the sorts of variable which influence such research. The chapter will conclude by considering the causal status of strategies, and finally their scope for application.

Generalizations about strategies

If we are to suggest that strategies influence language learning success, we need a framework or view of learning within which to locate such studies. The discussion will be organized around the relationship of strategies to (a) processes of language learning, (b) methods of increasing exposure to language learning and interaction, and (c) the management of learning.

Processes can be of two sorts – linguistic and cognitive. Although it is difficult to distinguish between these unequivocally, one could claim that the emphasis within strategy research has been towards the cognitive processing of information. There are exceptions to this, such as Rubin and Bialystok's work on inference, inductive and deductive reasoning, which might have a linguistic orientation, and the GLL study mentions the 'strategy' of attending to the systematic nature of language. But these are exceptions. In the main, linguistic processes have not been the *forte* of strategies researchers. Perhaps this is just as well, since it may be that linguistic processes are least amenable to intervention, with universal processes exerting a powerful constraining influence. There is also Seliger's (1983) criticism of a strategies methodology being applied to material which is difficult or impossible to access. Still, one must recognize that if strategies research is unable to probe linguistic processes, a very significant part of language learning is omitted from the research agenda, and the potential for comprehensive explanations thereby diminished.

The emphasis on cognitive process strategies perhaps reflects the hope that such strategies will be more amenable to study and intervention. There is, indeed, some systematicity. Strategies which involve simple operations on linguistic material, such as repetition and memorization, or the use of formulaic language, seem to be the first acquired (Chesterfield *et al.* 1985) and are the most frequently used in secondary school classrooms (O'Malley *et al.* 1985a). More sophisticated strategies such as elaboration, monitoring, or grouping, etc., which involve the transformation of material emerge later (Chesterfield *et al.* 1985) and are employed less frequently. Perhaps the simpler strategies are available to all, and training can influence their frequency and appropriateness of use. The more complex strategies may not be available to everyone, and their use may have to be explicitly taught to some students. If so, the use of metacognitive strategies, the most exciting development in recent strategy research, may not translate directly into easy application, since such strategies may be the most demanding of all to teach to students and implement effectively. The specific and non-generalizable strategies, that is, may be easier to work with but less interesting than the general and more abstract but more interesting ones.

This, in turn, connects with the issue of the conditions of learning. There is some evidence that the best studied strategies, and the ones that have the clearest effect, are performance based. Hosenfeld's (1977) work with reading, for example, seems to have been effective in modifying a word-based approach to reading, and inculcating the habit of clause, sentence, and even paragraph-based processing strategies. O'Malley *et al.* (1985a, b), in their training study, report a significant effect for the metacognitive strategy of analysing the communicative requirements of a speaking task. In each of these cases the strategy concerned had an immediate and direct influence on performance. One wonders whether the most trainable of strategies are those which have the quickest return. Possibly the less trainable strategies are those associated with aspects of language learning and cognitive *processes*, and whose effects can only be observed if they are used over extended periods of time. We clearly need to study the conditions of strategy modification more extensively. We can only claim to have scratched the surface so far and will need to study a range of different strategies under a range of different learning conditions before we can offer any serious generalizations about trainability in this area.

Having looked at process-based strategies, we can now turn to input, time, and interaction maximizing strategies. These did not figure prominently in work by Rubin and O'Malley but were fundamental for Naiman *et al.* (1978) and Wong-Fillmore (1979), and, to a certain extent, the Chesterfield *et al.* (1985) research. In these cases, the observational and retrospective data suggested that successful learners spent more time learning, ensured that they were exposed to more of the target language, and forced themselves or naturally entered into situations where they interacted with target language speakers. It would be interesting to obtain more controlled data on this issue, to see whether this predisposition is linked to motivational pattern (e.g. integratively motivated learners use strategies to maximize contact), or whether stable personality dispositions are involved, or indeed whether some people devise methods of overcoming diffidence about interaction opportunities. It also seems important here to link strategies to learning situations. The O'Malley *et al.* (1985a, b) studies emphasized strategies which were useful for classroom learning, and which were relevant for processing material presented in a formal context. Research such as that from the GLL study, based in naturalistic learning conditions, emphasized contact-inducing strategies. Clearly, what is relevant as a strategy varies from situation to situation, and research will have to take this into account.

A third group of strategies are broadly concerned with the management of the learning experience. In the GLL study several successful learners emphasized the management of *affective* aspects of learning. It has been interesting, more recently, to see the emphasis on the management of *cognitive* aspects of learning. These, for O'Malley *et al.* (1985a), involve issues like organizing one's attention and monitoring and evaluating one's performance. Wenden (1983) emphasizes the learner's capacity to analyse his needs, to plan, and to set priorities. In each case, we have an image of a learner thinking about his own learning, and making choices which seem, to him, to be optimal. This capacity, in turn, enables behaviour to be modified. There are connections here with attribution theory, from the last chapter, since the learner has a defence against viewing success as resulting from the fixed factor of ability, but instead can look upon it as influenced by effort whose direction can be altered.

Important variables in strategies research

In the main, strategies researchers have simply gathered data. It may be, however, that there are systematic relationships between other IDs and a predisposition to use certain strategies. We have just seen how an attributional analysis of motivation may be linked to management strategies. One might similarly relate the motivational orientations to strategies, e.g. with integratively oriented learners being more likely to use such strategies. Similarly, aptitudinal characteristics might connect with the type of metacognitive and cognitive strategies that are used, e.g. memory-dependent learners using memorization strategies, analytic learners tending more towards inference and deductive strategies.

Another variable which may be connected to strategy use is age. We currently have to deal with studies which have not systematically covered the age range of learners. Wong-Fillmore (1979) and Chesterfield and Chesterfield (1985) looked at very young children at school entry age; O'Malley *et al.* (1985a, b) studied secondary (high) schoolchildren; and Politzer and McGroarty (1985), Naiman *et al.* (1978), Rubin (1981), Huang and Van Naerssen (1985), and Bialystok (1979) researched with university students and other adults. Strategies may vary simply as a function of age. Certainly the O'Malley (1985a) research has revealed enormously greater scope for metacognitive abilities by secondary school age. A final variable which might influence strategy findings is that of proficiency level. Naiman *et al.* (1978) looked at very advanced adult learners while at the other extreme the Chesterfields (1985) studied young, fairly low proficiency children. One has the impression that other investigators, necessarily perhaps, are somewhere between these two extremes. It may well be that different strategies are differentially appropriate at different levels of proficiency.

The causal status of strategies

We saw, in Chapter 4, that one can argue that motivation is the result, not a cause. One can similarly argue that learner strategies do not determine proficiency, *but are permitted by it*. The use of learner strategies, that is, may not lead to higher accomplishments – instead one of the benefits of higher proficiency may be the capacity to use a wider range of strategies. The Huang and Van Naerssen (1985) study exemplifies this problem. Significant differences in reported strategy use were found between the top and bottom third of a group of students. Since the research design was cross-sectional we do not know whether the strategies came first, and had brought about the proficiency level, or that those who were more proficient, for whatever reason, accordingly had the potential to use strategies. Only a longitudinal research design which monitors changes in strategies and proficiency over time in the same group of learners can address this issue. At present, with the exception of the Wong-Fillmore (1982) and Chesterfield and Chesterfield (1985) work with very young children, we do not have any examples of such research designs.

Learner training and intervention

There has been a progressive trend in recent years towards individualized instruction (Geddes and Sturtridge 1982; Altman and James 1980), and with this has come a desire to give the learner greater responsibility for his own learning. Learner training seeks to help the learner in this move towards decision-making and autonomy by providing a structure for the choices that are made (Dickenson 1987). Very frequently, strategy research provides input for the training suggestions that are made, as exemplified, for example, in Ellis and Sinclair (1987). Similarly, some of the broad categorizations of strategies (e.g. in

O'Malley *et al.* 1985a) have been strongly influenced by issues in autonomous learning. Wenden (1983, 1986, 1987a) has researched how learners think about their own learning, how they represent decisions about learning to themselves, and what aspects of their learning they can most readily describe. She emphasizes the questions that learners could ask themselves to help *define* the problem of language learning, especially in relation to self-evaluation, and an ability to analyse why one has or has not made progress. She also focuses upon how learners could be helped to plan their learning, and to set priorities for themselves. We saw in Chapter 3 that one feature of language aptitude concerns the ability to impose structure on learning, and for learners to use their time effectively, especially when decontextualized aspects of language learning are concerned. Work on learner training such as Wenden's seems to be providing a sort of scaffolding for learners who have difficulty in establishing such a structure for themselves. It is to be hoped that in the future the product of such learner-strategy research can be useful in deciding on the form of intervention programmes that are most appropriate. At present many of the features of such intervention programmes are based on work done in other areas (e.g. reading: Brown and Palinscar 1982) or informed supposition. Learner-strategy research should have an important role in establishing an empirical basis for the components of such intervention programmes in the future.

Learner strategies: conclusions

If, now, we review the whole of the learner-strategies research, we have to say that the area is at an embryonic stage. Conflicting results and methodologies proliferate. There are few hard findings. Even the causal role and intervention potential of strategies could be disputed. We seem, that is, to be dealing with a clear example of a research-then-theory perspective, in which there is no established framework for the research which has been conducted, and in which different investigators 'trawl' in different ways. Yet the area of research has considerable attractions. A lot of useful and suggestive research has now been reported. There are the beginnings of systematicity in the categorization schemes for strategies, so that new investigators need not gather information blindly. The metacognitive/cognitive/cooperative general categories seem useful in a fairly direct way for school based learning. Given Wenden's work (e.g. 1983) they would also seem to have potential for informal learning environments, especially if supplemented by other global categories concerned with input and interaction maximization. This suggests that we are ready for (a) the first attempts at theorizing within the learner-strategies field which should account for the interrelationships between strategies, and the extent of their causal role in learning, and (b) the development of more replicable and public research techniques, including, perhaps, more examples of questionnaire measures.

6

Additional cognitive and affective influences on language learning

In contrast to the preceding three chapters which have each focused on one major theme, this chapter will examine a diverse collection of cognitive and affective influences. In most cases these are derived from work in mainstream psychology, and then adapted for language learning. Accordingly, each section begins with a brief attempt to ground the trait in general psychological functioning before considering specifically language-related studies.

Extroversion–introversion

Eysenck (1965), provides the following portraits of introverts and extroverts:

> The typical extrovert is sociable, likes parties, has many friends, needs to have people to talk to, and does not like studying by himself. He craves excitement, takes chances, often sticks his neck out, acts on the spur of the moment, and is generally an impulsive individual. He . . . always has a ready answer, and generally likes change . . .

> The typical introvert, on the other hand, is a quiet, retiring sort of person, introspective, fond of books rather than people; he is reserved and distant, except with intimate friends. He tends to plan ahead . . . and distrusts the impulse of the moment. He does not like excitement, takes matters of everyday life with proper seriousness, and likes a well ordered mode of life . . . (pp.59–60)

Basically, extroversion seems to consist of two component – sociability (i.e. gregariousness, people-orientation, fear of isolation) and impulsivity (need for excitement and change, for risk taking). Eysenck is proposing that these two components go together, i.e. sociable people also tend to be impulsive. Eysenck (1957) suggests that extroverts will be easily distracted from studying, partly as a result of their gregariousness and partly because of an inability to concentrate for long periods. In relation to this latter problem, Eysenck, working within a conditioning framework, suggests that extroverts build up reactive inhibition (or fatigue) to learning more quickly, a suggestion backed up by some laboratory experiments on learning. Entwistle and Wilson (1977) even suggest, on the basis of some studies that show extroverts having superior immediate recall, but poorer recall after a delay (Eysenck 1970), that introverts may code material more efficiently into long-term memory. In view of all these findings, it has been predicted that introverts will have higher academic achievement than extroverts.

In general, educational research is supportive of the above interpretation. There is a tendency for extroverts to underperform slightly compared to introverts. Entwistle and Entwistle (1970), for example, report a correlation of 0.25 between extroversion and academic success amongst British university students. They also found that introversion was associated with good study methods, but introversion still correlated significantly with achievement even when the effect of the good study methods was removed.

An extremely interesting aspect of applied linguistic research is that the desirable end of the extroversion–introversion continuum has been taken to be extroversion. Many investigators (e.g. Naiman *et al.*, 1978; McDonough 1981) have suggested that more sociable learners will be more inclined to talk, more inclined to join groups, more likely to participate in class, more likely to volunteer and to engage in practice activities, and finally, more likely to maximize language-use opportunities outside the classroom by using language for communication. Thus extroverts would benefit both inside and outside classrooms by having the appropriate personality trait for *language* learning (as distinct from general, content-oriented learning) since such learning is best accomplished, according to most theorists, by actually *using* language. Extroverts would be likely to maximize contact and the quantity of input received (Krashen 1985); maximize interaction (Long 1985), assuming negotiating meaning through interaction is crucial; and maximize language output (Swain 1985), assuming that the process of using language is important for development.

We see, then, something of a conflict between *general* learning predictions in this area, and *language* learning predictions. If we turn from theorizing to a review of the actual research results that are available, one has to say that the situation is not clear cut. Pritchard (1952) reported a correlation of 0.92 between sociability and ratings of French fluency amongst British grammar school students. However the research design of the study has been severely criticized. Gardner (1985) notes that both measures involved in this correlation were ratings (of fluency and playground activity) made by the same three people (including the experimenter). The possibility of contamination cannot therefore be ruled out. The narrowness and subjectivity of the criterion measure also warrant comment. Chastain (1975) also examined correlations between sociability and achievement amongst college students of French, Spanish and German. He obtained four relevant correlations between a reserved–outgoing scale, and grades. Two of these were significant, providing correlations between 0.30 and 0.34, while two correlations did not attain significance. There is evidence, therefore, of a weak and rather uncertain relationship, accounting for, at best, 10 per cent of the variance on the criterion measure. In contrast, Smart *et al.* (1970) did not find any positive relationship between extroversion/sociability and college language achievement, even suggesting that a group of over-achievers (relative to the achievement predicted on the basis of high-school grades and academic aptitude) were characterized by a tendency to be introverted, i.e. what distinguished this group from a group attaining 'predicted' achievement was that the achievers preferred to work alone, and to avoid group-oriented activities. On the other hand, Rossier (1976) found a positive relationship between extroversion and oral fluency (note that fluency was the criterion for the positive correlation found by Pritchard 1952) but this relationship did not hold up for other proficiency tests. Swain and Burnaby (1976) did not find any significant relationships between teacher ratings of personality attributes and performance of either immersion or regular language course students. Genessee and Hamayan (1980) also failed to find any positive relationships between personality variables and achievement. Similarly, Ely (1986) in a more complex design in which sociability was hypothesized to be a component predictor of classroom participation (which was itself meant to be a component predictor of proficiency), found that sociability did *not* predict classroom participation, and that, in any case, classroom participation only predicted one of three criterion measures, a 'correctness' factor based on a story-retelling task. Finally, Strong (1983) did not find a relationship between a measure of extroversion (based on the Early School Personality Questionnaire (Coan and Cattell 1966)) and various indices of structure, vocabulary and pronunciation, based on the naturalistic language obtained from a group of kindergarteners in a California school.

Strong (1983) provides a table grouping the studies of extroversion in terms of the test-type used, and whether positive or negative relationships were found. An amended version of the table is reproduced below. For each study, information is given on whether adults or children were involved; whether the learning setting was naturalistic or FL; and the nature of the measuring instrument used.

The table is not totally systematic, but there are some generalizations that can be made. There is a very slight tendency for positive relationships to be associated with the type of measuring instrument used. When NCL measures are involved, five positive versus four non-relationships result. In contrast, for LTL, non-relationships outnumber the positive ones, four to two. There are stronger tendencies for positive relationships to be more likely with naturalistic as opposed to FL learning situations; with children, and especially young children, as opposed to adults; and with observationally based assessments of personality disposition, as opposed to questionnaire-derived measures. This last variable seems to be the most important of all: every observational study produces a positive relationship, while the questionnaire studies tend to produce non-relationships.

It would appear, therefore, that a positive relationship can be demonstrated, but that the appearance of such a relationship is somewhat dependent on research design decisions. It seems reasonable to conclude also, in view of the small size of correlations reported, that even when research design decisions favourable to this appearance are made, we are looking at a fairly weak relationship which accounts for only a small proportion of the variance on criterion measures.

Two directions for further research are suggested by these conclusions. First, we need research which attends more rigorously to contextual factors. In this respect some general educational research reported by Wankowski (1973) is interesting. He related extroversion/introversion to age, and found that below puberty extroversion tends to have a positive relationship with achievement, whereas after puberty introverts are more successful. He related this switch to the changed nature of the learning tasks involved. Prior to puberty classes are often organized on a group basis. Subsequently, subject specialism makes individual work, including homework, more important. As a result, the 'achieving personality' may change, depending on the learning environment. This, quite clearly, is relevant for language teaching. As an area of learning, it is more concerned with group activities, especially where communicative approaches are used. We should expect, therefore, that language learning should show a more sustained effect for extroversion. However, the crucial issue now becomes one of understanding the *process* of learning. In earlier chapters it has been argued that, even in naturalistic environments, there are aspects of learning which go beyond learning-by-doing, and talking to learn. The analytic capacities from the aptitude studies support this claim, as do the aspects of learner strategies that reflect self-awareness on the part of learners, planning, monitoring, and systematicity on their part about the learning task that confronts them. These aspects of learning would seem to relate more easily to the introvert. As a result, we may need to accept that extroversion and introversion each have their positive features, and that an extreme either way is likely to work against some aspects of target-language development. There is value, it would seem, in having rather variable personality qualities, so that one can adapt effectively to meet different learning demands.

The second direction for future research concerns an improved definition of the constructs involved. Eysenck's original pen-portrait of extroversion seemed to imply two underlying dimensions – of sociability and impulsivity. In language learning, one can see potential relationships for sociability but not really for impulsivity and a craving for excitement. (Risk-taking will be discussed below.) In other words, there are grounds for questioning the desirability of adopting, wholesale, a construct from a feeder discipline, psychology, rather than subjecting the construct to further analysis to relate it specifically to language learning.

Some investigators have indeed attempted to produce measures which are more fine-grained and relevant. A good example of this is Strong's work (1983) where the overall construct of social style is broken down into talkativeness (i.e. tendency to initiate conversations), responsiveness, gregariousness (i.e. the tendency to interact with a wide number of peers), assertiveness, extroversion, social competence and popularity. These measures were correlated with three criterion scores; for structural knowledge, vocabulary and pronunciation, with all measures based on a naturalistically obtained sample of language. The results obtained are shown in Table 6.2.

Table 6.2: Correlations of social styles with language measures

	TALK	RESP	GREG	ASST	EXTR	SCMP	POP
NCL Str	.72*	.65*	.50	.18	.31	.62*	.04
NCL Voc	.72*	.82*	.67*	.42	− .21	.38	.05
NCL Pro	.52*	.73*	.43	.18	.04	.40	.01

* = p < .05

Note: NCL = Natural communicative language   TALK = Talkativeness
     Str = Productive structural knowledge   RESP = Responsiveness
     Voc = Play vocabulary   GREG = Gregariousness
     Pro = Pronunciation   ASST = Assertiveness
     EXTR = Extroversion   SCMP = Social competence
     POP = Popularity

These correlations are based on a sample of only 13 kindergarteners, and so they need to be interpreted circumspectly. However, the consistency is striking. The measures which generate significant correlations are Talkativeness and Responsiveness, both reflections of willingness to enter into conversations. Assertiveness, Extroversion, and

Popularity produce not one significant correlation between them, while Gregariousness and Social Competence produce only one each. It would seem, from these results, that it is the sociability dimension of extroversion that is relevant for language learning, rather than impulsivity. Further, it seems to be specifically the tendency to engage in verbal interactions which, when separated out from the other components of extroversion, is most predictive. It would be interesting to attempt to confirm this result with a larger sample of children; with adults; with a wider range of criterion measures; with a more diverse set of operationalizations of the different sub-constructs within extroversion; and in FL settings in contrast to naturalistic ones. This might clarify the operation of the variables concerned.

Risk-taking

It has also been proposed that a tendency to take risks is associated with greater language learning success. Beebe (1983), in a review of the area, follows Bem (1971) by relating risk-taking to the situation, the social setting, and the individual. We will focus only on the last of these, given the present emphasis on IDs. Here the main issue, in terms of general psychology, is whether there is a stable personality attribute of 'risk-taking'. McClelland (1958, 1961, McClelland *et al*. 1953) developed a theory of achievement motivation which proposes that some learners perceive the likelihood of achieving goals as constituting medium-risk tasks, and respond to such challenges on the basis of a past history of success with such tasks. In contrast, other learners will be attracted by low *or* high-risk tasks. Low-risk tasks will be easily achievable, but as a result, unmotivating, since they constitute no real accomplishment. The theory proposes that successful learners, other things being equal, will be those who construe the tasks that face them as medium-risk, and achievable. As a result, they are more likely to engage in the cumulative learning activities that lead to longer-term success. Unsuccessful learners, on the other hand, will tend to be those who set excessively high or low goals for themselves, with neither of these outcomes likely to lead to sustained learning.

Within the ESOL field, there has been a less finely drawn account of the role of risk-taking. Risk-taking has been seen as generally and pervasively good. Two areas stand out in this. First of all, risk-taking in situations containing social interaction has been seen as likely to increase opportunities to hear language (and obtain input), and to speak language (and use output and engage in functional practice) (cf. the earlier discussion on extroversion). This view of risk-taking would relate nicely to the Good Language Learner research. The second area where risk-taking might be important is in the actual language that is used. If development involves the growth of a structured linguistic system, and this can only proceed through hypothesis formation and hypothesis testing, then the successful learner is more likely to be one who takes his existing language system to the limit, and tries out risky hypotheses where feedback will be most revealing. Such a risk-taking language learner is similar to Popper's 'bold scientist'. One imagines adventurous learners being more likely to change, also more resistant to fossilization.

There are problems when we try to relate general psychological theories to work on risk-taking specifically within ESOL. First of all, there is the decision as to how stable a risk-taking propensity is. The implication from the McClelland–Atkinson position is that people can be, to some extent, depended upon in terms of whether they are low or high risk takers, on the one hand, or medium-risk takers, on the other. However, it is possible that situational factors may influence the operation of IDs here. Beebe (1983), for example, considers whether tasks involve skill or chance; whether people have different value systems to assess rewards; and the influence of prior experience. The conclusion seems to be that there is no simple generalization about risk-taking stability in the face of these factors. In ESOL particularly the problem is to decide whether people vary in their social risk-taking from situation to situation. Is the timid learner in one situation likely to be quite venturesome in another? Do people vary from day to day, from mood to mood, in terms of how adventurous they are with language structure hypotheses? We need to know, that is, whether we are dealing with behaviour which is influenced by a risk-taking propensity or alternatively whether we are dealing with social habits. Perhaps it is simply personality variables, e.g. extroversion, that are the dominant factor, and that consistency comes, not from evaluations of the risks in situations, so much as force of habit in social situations as a result of personality dispositions.

A second general issue is that of the external validity of the risk-taking research. The McClelland–Atkinson theory, and the various forms of Attribution Theory, are largely based on investigations in psychological laboratories in which subjects (often psychology undergraduates fulfilling course requirements) agreed to participate in certain tasks involving risk-taking behaviour. Most of this research involves out-of-context behaviour, on tasks of no integral significance for the subjects, and on a 'one-off' basis. Quite clearly, generalization to cumulative, real learning needs to be with care. As a result, there is no sense in which the psychological 'results' can be the basis for direct application in ESOL. The hypotheses may have been generated more quickly: they now need to be re-validated.

We now turn to the actual research which has been carried out on risk-taking within ESOL. One interesting study is that of Ely. He

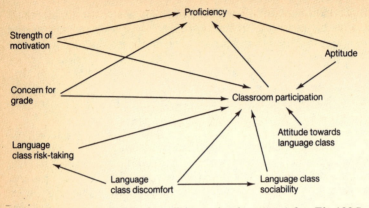

Figure 6.1: Ely's model of proficiency development (after Ely 1986)

proposed the underlying model shown in Figure 6.1.

It can be seen that classroom participation is hypothesized to influence proficiency directly (as are class discomfort, sociability, etc.) and to reflect the contributing influences of risk-taking, discomfort, sociability, etc. So at one level classroom participation is a dependent variable, predicted by other variables in turn, while at another level, it is, itself, an independent variable, hypothesized to be predictive of proficiency. It also needs to be mentioned that there are some variables such as aptitude and motivation which are thought to influence both classroom participation and proficiency.

Ely (1986) assessed classroom risk-taking with a six-item scale. Some examples are given below.

1 I like to wait until I know exactly how to use a Spanish word before using it (–)
4 I prefer to say what I want to say in Spanish without worrying about the small details of grammar.
6 I prefer to follow basic sentence models rather than risk misusing the language. (–)

The original scale had contained 12 items, and the six which were used were those which survived an item-analysis cycle. The original 12-item scale had aimed to sample the four dimensions that Ely proposes underlie the risk-taking construct:

1 a lack of hesitancy about using a newly encountered linguistic element
2 a willingness to use linguistic elements perceived to be complex or difficult
3 a tolerance of possible incorrectness or inexactitude in using the language

4 an inclination to rehearse a new element silently before attempting to use it aloud.

The six items retained did, in fact, sample each of these dimensions, but obviously the brevity of the scale placed a considerable weight on each item. Classroom participation was operationalized as the number of times a student volunteered to participate in class, i.e. by asking or answering a question or providing information in Spanish without being asked. Finally, proficiency was measured by a story-retelling task evaluated in terms of (a) oral correctness, (b) oral fluency, and (c) a written correctness score based on the students' final examination.

Ely (1986) reports two important results. First, there was a correlation of 0.39 between the risk-taking scale and classroom participation (p < .01), i.e. high scorers on the risk-taking scale did tend to volunteer more in class. Second, the association between classroom participation and proficiency was examined using two groups of students (at slightly different levels), and three tests, generating six correlations in all. One of these was significant. The lower-level students showed a correlation of 0.40 between the oral correctness score for the story-retelling task and classroom participation. The other correlations were generally very low. As a result, we are faced with a slender and indirect relationship between risk-taking and language learning success. We evidently have some way to go in the risk-taking area before anything comparable to conclusions about extroversion–introversion can be drawn. Consequently, the speculations about the role of risk-taking in language learning that one frequently reads need to be interpreted with caution.

Intelligence

In the aptitude chapter we saw that to justify the concept of foreign language aptitude we have to be able to show it is different from intelligence. This relationship has been investigated, somewhat in passing, by a number of researchers, and in detail by a major study by Wesche, Edwards and Wells (1982). The less-focused research generally included intelligence measures within an aptitude battery. Typical correlations between intelligence and aptitude from these studies are 0.41 (Gardner and Lambert 1972: IQ with Words in Sentences, Pt 4 of the MLAT), and 0.39 (Skehan 1980: IQ with MLAT Pt 4). Such figures indicate 16% of shared variance. Since the correlations in each case are significant, it is clear that there is a relationship between aptitude and intelligence, but the rather low proportion of shared variance also suggests a considerable degree of independence. Skehan (1980) also attempted to assess the aptitude–intelligence relationship more selectively. He included a verbal IQ measure in an aptitude battery and factor-analysed the results. Three major factors emerged. The first of these was defined, on the basis of the tests which loaded highly, as an analytic capacity with verbal materials. The verbal intelligence test had a loading of 0.30 on this factor, suggesting that verbal intelligence relates most strongly to the analytic capacity of language aptitude.

Wesche *et al.* (1982) report an extensive study directed specifically at the relationship between aptitude and intelligence. Subjects were administered the MLAT (all five sub-tests) and Thurstone and Thurstone's (1965) Primary Mental Abilities test (PMA). The PMA gives separate scores for Verbal Meaning, Number Facility, Reasoning, and Spatial Relations. The overall correlation between the MLAT and PMA was 0.67, accounting for 45 per cent of common variance.

Looking at the results from the perspective of individual tests, 'the best single predictor of all the variables taken together is the measure of general reasoning, or the ability to reason using words and numbers, that is, with symbols.' The reasoning test had a squared multiple correlation (SMC), indicating shared variance, of 0.58. However, three of the MLAT tests (Number Learning, Phonetic Script, and Paired Associates) have much lower SMCs, suggesting that there is more unique variance associated with them, i.e. that phonemic coding ability and memory, the factors implicated here, may be more independent of intelligence. Finally, MLAT Spelling Clues seems to be associated with the PMA Verbal Meaning test, suggesting a slightly different aspect of the intelligence–aptitude relationship, this time in terms of first-language verbal stock.

Wesche *et al.* (1982) also report the results of some factor analyses. Two different factor-analytic solutions are proposed. The first, based on a Varimax rotation after a principal-factors analysis (cf. Chapter 2) suggests three factors, defined respectively by (i) MLAT Spelling Clues and PMA Verbal Meaning (*Language Verbal Knowledge*); (ii) all the remaining PMA tests (*Abstract Reasoning Ability*); (iii) all the remaining MLAT tests, with slightly higher loadings for Paired Associates and Number Learning (*Language Learning Abilities, especially memory*). The second (and related) solution suggested the possibility of correlation between the different factors. The same three factors emerged, but only after a general factor had been extracted, i.e. these same three factors were secondary in importance to the general factor. Wesche *et al.* (1982) interpret this solution in terms of a hierarchical model of intelligence (Vernon 1961) with a general, pervasive intelligence factor supplemented by various specifics.

It would seem therefore that intelligence and aptitude are related to one another, and that one can interpret language aptitude as consisting of specific components of intelligence which are especially relevant to learning situations. However, some qualifications are necessary. This conclusion is nothing like as clear-cut for the phonemic coding ability and memory tests as it is for the language analytic ability tests. In addition, the Bristol follow up research has argued for some degree of independence between language analytic capacity and other aspects of cognitive functioning. One can also add that the factor-analytic investigations reported by Gardner and Lambert (1972) and Skehan (1982) do not offer such a clear picture as do those of Wesche *et al.* (1982) and report less common variance. In each of these other cases, a wider range of measures were included. It is possible, that is, that future factor-analytic investigations of the aptitude–intelligence relationship, based on a wider sampling of component measures, may not yield the same results. There is scope for such research.

Field independence and other cognitive abilities

More recently, there has also been interest in other cognitive abilities that might be relevant to the task of language learning. The principal such ability is field independence, although attention has also been paid to category width, and tolerance for ambiguity (Brown 1987). Field independence is a construct that derives from the work of the psychologist Witkin (1962, Witkin, Goodenough, and Oltman 1979). In its central form, it concerns visual perception and an individual's capacity to separate figure from ground in an illustration. It is assessed by the Embedded Figures Test (Witkin, Oltman, Raskin and Karp 1971) in which the subject has to find a target shape embedded in a more complex pattern. The test is hypothesized to reflect the way individuals perceive and organize the world. People who do well on the test (Field Independent (FI) individuals) are thought to be able to separate figures from ground, to separate the essential from the inessential, and to be usefully analytic. People who do poorly on the test (Field Dependent people), on the other hand, see the world as an unanalysed whole, and do not tend to attend to any part of it selectively. So far, field independence has been restricted to cognitive functioning. Witkin *et al.* (1979) see its operation as wider-ranging, and also important in the area of personality. Field-dependent individuals are thought to be person-oriented, interested in other people and sensitive to them, indeed some investigators prefer the term 'field sensitive' individuals. They are also thought to be outgoing and gregarious. In contrast, field-independent learners are more impersonal and detached, less sensitive and more aloof; they are cerebral and object-oriented.

The field-independence construct, although originally from the field of perception, has also been related to language learning. Field-dependent learners, it is proposed, as a result of their person-orientation, will be more inclined to interpersonal situations, wanting contact with other people, and engaging in verbal interaction with them. This should lead to greater communicative competence, greater conversational resourcefulness, greater negotiation skill, etc., all of which should be beneficial for exposure to language and therefore language development through interaction. But one of the appealing aspects of the field-(in)dependence construct is that it is not one-directional in its effects: field-independent people have their advantages, too, in terms of language learning. Given the internal orientation of FIs, they are supposed to have greater analytic and cognitive restructuring capabilities. 'Fields', which may be internal *or* external, can be broken up, re-analysed, and reassembled more easily, with new bases for the organization of the field being tried out. In language learning terms, the FI description would seem relevant for resistance to fossilization, and for the capacity to restructure and develop interlanguage systems more readily.

The preceding paragraphs, then, have tried to provide a rationale for the extension of the field-independence construct from general psychology to language learning. The chain of argument is very appealing, but the extension of application needs to be justified. Two lines of research are crucial to support the claims made. *Convergent validation* needs to establish that basically the same construct is involved in the different domains in which FI is supposed to operate. *Discriminant validation* needs to establish that the construct 'field-independence' is not a redundant one, already covered by other constructs, and not simply duplicating their operation.

Quite a lot of research has now been conducted within the ESOL area. In the main, studies have used a similar format. A group of language learners has been administered a version of the Embedded Figures Test, and then correlations have been computed between scores on the EFT and scores on criterion tests. A number of studies have also included other predictor tests besides EFT, but, interestingly enough, the level of analysis has usually been correlational, rather than factor-analytic, so that the emphasis has usually been on first-order relationships, rather than the internal structure of the predictor measures. In other words, these studies have not really addressed the convergent and discriminant validation criteria discussed in Chapter 2.

Naiman *et al*. (1978) found a significant correlation between field independence and performance on a French oral production test and on a French listening comprehension test. The subjects were 72 Grade 8, 10 and 12 children receiving conventional French as a foreign language instruction. Two things are of note. First, the correlations, although significant, were not strong (0.31 with a standardized listening test and 0.25 with an imitation test). Second, despite the rationale for the construct, field *in*dependence (not dependence), correlated with an *oral* (i.e. imitation-type task), rather against the direction of prediction, since one would expect Field Dependence to correlate with the more communication-oriented tests, and Field Independence with the more cognitive tests. Genessee and Hamayan (1980) reported significant correlations between EFT and performance on a general achievement test in French and listening comprehension test but not for an oral production test for a group of six- to seven-year-old children participating in a French immersion programme. The correlations, once again, were rather low: 0.35 for general French achievement, 0.31 for listening comprehension, and 0.10 with oral production. Further, in a factor analysis, the EFT test loaded highly on a factor which seemed to involve non-verbal reasoning.

In contrast, Bialystok and Frohlich (1977, 1978) did not find any significant correlations in a study they ran with 14- and 15-year-old students. These investigators suggested that the FI construct has only a minor role in language learning. Tucker *et al.* (1976) also failed to find a relationship between FI and performance on listening comprehension, reading comprehension, or oral production tests, but did find a relationship with an achievement test of general language skills. Reves (1982), similarly, found essentially near-zero relationships between two measures of field-independence (verbal FI and non-verbal FI) and criterion scores with Arab learners of English (in a formal setting) and Hebrew (in an informal setting). We can conclude, from this research, that the relationship between FI and language learning success is, at best, weak, and at worst, non-existent, in that the occasional significant correlations may involve a large component of chance.

Some investigators have attempted to establish discriminant validity for FI. As a preliminary to reviewing this work, it is useful to examine a table of different continua of several of the constructs posited to be important within an ID framework.

Table 6.3:   Some ID distinctions

Field independent ---	Field dependent
Bright --	Dull
Analytic learner --	Formulaic learner
Introvert --	Extrovert
Rule learners ---	Data-gatherers
Low sociability ---	High sociability

The problem is that in many of these cases, the different sets of terms have close relationships to one another. Some of the qualities of the field-dependent learners, such as sensitivity and person-orientation are also captured by other constructs such as extroversion and sociability. Qualities of the FI learner such as capacity to analyse, to separate field from ground, seem close to those associated with the analytic learner identified by the aptitude research, and to aspects of intelligence. The obvious research procedure here is to try and develop measures of each of these constructs, and establish their separateness from one another, as well as their respective relationships with criterion scores. This would allow us to decide which abilities are central to language learning, and which are merely 'hanging on the coat tails' of others.

In fact, very little such research has been conducted. The one exception to this is the relationship between intelligence and FI. It has been proposed, that is, that field-independence works because it is a surrogate measure of intelligence. If one removed the influence of intelligence from FI measures, this argument runs, there would be no significant relationship left. This was the research strategy adopted by Hansen and Stansfield (1981). They administered the EFT to a group of 300 first semester college Spanish students, together with tests of linguistic, communicative and integrative competence. These criterion measures were then correlated with the EFT scores, producing correlations ranging from 0.20 to 0.43, with a median correlation of around 0.24 (all significant correlations). The associations therefore seemed weak to moderate but real. (See also the discussion in Chapter 2 of the interpretation of low but significant correlations.) But Hansen and Stansfield (1981) were concerned to eliminate general attainment as a disguised influence on the first-order correlations, and so they partialled out scholastic ability. When this was done, only one of the total of six criterion tests still entered into a significant relationship, i.e. an integrative test, cloze, which still had a correlation, after scholastic ability had been partialled out, of 0.22.

These results were replicated in a study by L. Hansen (1984). The subjects were 15- to 19-year-old students from six Pacific Island cultures. Once again, significant correlations between EFT and language measures were found, and once again, these ranged, for the whole sample, between 0.21 and 0.42 (similar figures to Hansen and Stansfield 1981), all of which were significant. (There was considerable variation in the coefficients obtained in the different island cultures, with many non-significant correlations (34 out of 47 correlations were non-significant at the sub-group level) suggesting that these results, as Hansen notes, should be interpreted cautiously.) Once again, however, when scholastic ability was partialled out in a sub-sample of the subjects (the sub-sample which had, incidentally, produced the highest first-order correlations between EFT and language scores), the correlations were no longer, except in one case out of eight, significant.

We have to conclude, therefore, that the studies that have been conducted into the relationship of field-independence and language learning success, which have between them covered a wide range of subject types and instructional conditions, have demonstrated, at best, a weak relationship, and often, no relationship at all. Worse, there are strong grounds for believing that field-independence only works when it is a disguised measure of intelligence, and it is the intelligence component of the test that accounts for the result. Interesting though the underlying hypothesis may be, the research results are not encouraging. Field-Independence looks to be a seam which has been mined for all the value that is going to be found.

Anxiety

Eysenck (1970) talks of the neurotic personality as a worrier, moody, restless and generally anxious. He views the anxious or neurotic person as one who does things to reduce such stress, a characterization which would seem to imply a positive correlation with achievement, since anxiety level could be the source, the fuel, for a drive to remove the cause for worry. However, three immediate complications to this picture present themselves. First of all, there is the possibility of a non-linear relationship between anxiety and performance (Scovel 1978). Some anxiety (relative to no anxiety) may be beneficial and energizing, i.e. a nice amount of stimulation for activity. Excessive anxiety, on the other hand, may cause activity with insufficient purpose, activity for its own sake, with learners repeatedly engaging in the same, unproductive activities. A second problem with the favourable interpretation of anxiety is that different people handle anxiety in different ways. Even if we assume that anxiety causes stress, and that learners will then do things to reduce stress, there is no guarantee that all learners will direct their energies in educationally desirable ways. Rather than do the homework which is a source of worry, some students might engage in escapist activity, or even cut class (Bailey 1983). Finally, one can make a distinction between a general anxiety trait, which affects behaviour in all domains (the indiscriminate neurotic), and anxiety states which result from exposure to specific situations, e.g. a specific teacher or a specific communicative situation. This problem of general vs. specific anxiety is particularly important when measurement is concerned, since it influences test and questionnaire content, as well as the scope for generalization.

Perhaps one final issue that has emerged from the general psychological literature is also worth mentioning. Spielberger (1962) has reported findings suggesting that the influence of anxiety changes as a function of ability level. He reports a tendency for anxiety to be facilitating in high-ability students, but that for low-ability students, and especially average-ability students, anxiety was associated with poor performance, and even failure (see also Scovel 1978). This finding raises the need to consider what is perhaps a fairly obvious point – the possibility that anxiety may partly be the *result* of low achievement. A related point, discussed by Scovel (1978), is that anxiety has different effects at different stages of learning, being more facilitating at higher levels, but debilitating at more beginning stages. Possibly higher-proficiency learners have a wider repertoire of behaviours which enable them to cope with anxiety-provoking situations more flexibly.

Early attempts within second langauge learning to establish a role for anxiety took what, in retrospect, was a fairly simplistic approach. General measures, derived from psychology, were administered to second language learners, and then correlated with criterion scores. Typical general trait approaches to anxiety were the Sarason Test Anxiety Scale (Sarason 1958) and the Taylor Manifest Anxiety Scale (Taylor 1953). Measures such as these failed to produce consistently significant correlations. Chastain (1975), for example, found significant negative correlations with his students of Spanish, but did not obtain significance with students of French and German. Using a slightly different framework (audience sensitivity) as a basis for anxiety, an early Gardner and Lambert (1959) study similarly failed to find significant associations between anxiety and language achievement.

More recently, investigators have tended to use measures of anxiety which are situation-specific, and which incorporate reference to the fact that it is a language that is being learned and used. It is hoped that the more specific contexts of the scale items used will be more likely to generate significant correlations. Hence items such as (from Gardner 1985, p. 179):

1 It embarrasses me to volunteer answers in our French class.
4 I get nervous and confused when I am speaking in my French class

and from Ely (1986):
1 I don't feel very relaxed when I speak Spanish in class.
4 I think I'm less self-conscious about actively participating in my Spanish class than most of the other students.

The above examples refer to language teaching classrooms. They focus on anxiety resulting from the public performance aspects of language learning. Bailey (1983) enumerates other possible sources of anxiety in ESOL as:

(a) Comparison of oneself with other students, either for their performance, or for their anxiety levels.
(b) One's relationship with the teacher, either in relation to one's perception of the teacher's expectations or one's need to gain the teacher's approval.
(c) Tests
(d) Comparison with oneself, and one's own personal standards and goals.

She also mentions influences such as one's competitiveness (as a factor likely to exacerbate the influence of any of the above factors), and one's feelings of solidarity and friendship with one's classmates (as a factor likely to reduce anxiety).

Gardner *et al*. (1976) have suggested that classroom anxiety is fairly consistently amongst the highest correlates with achievement (i.e. negative correlations), only being surpassed by aptitude and motivation. However, although 12 of the 15 correlations reported in the Gardner *et al*. (1976) study are significant, they are generally not very high, and account for relatively little variance in the criterion test scores. Gardner (1985) also suggests that older students have slightly higher levels of anxiety, suggesting that in addition to ability level and stage of learning, age of learner, too, may be an important variable in anxiety research. Ely (1986) also used the construct of anxiety in his research aimed at clarifying the antecedents of classroom participation (which was then seen as one of the antecedents of achievement). He developed a scale of Language Class Discomfort, meant to reflect the self-consciousness, anxiety and embarrassment learners experienced when taking part in a language class. This scale correlated at –0.27 with a measure of language classroom participation, suggesting a weak association such that anxious students are slightly less likely to participate in class. (Classroom participation itself correlated at 0.40 with one measure of proficiency.)

Gardner (1985) has also reported factor analyses which aim at clarifying the nature of the language anxiety construct. Several studies report an anxiety-linked factor, either based simply on anxiety measures, or more generally involving self-ratings of English competence, attitudes towards the English course, and indices of motivation to learn English. These more extended studies label the factor concerned 'self-confidence', and locate anxiety as one of its components. Such studies frequently make links (e.g. Clement *et al*. 1980) between situational anxiety and more general anxiety, suggesting that while it is valuable to have indicators of a specific language learning anxiety, this may often be related, to some degree, to a more generalized trait. However, these studies also sometimes find a lack of relationship between classroom anxiety and achievement. The correlation study mentioned earlier obtained some correlations which were non-significant. Similarly, Gardner *et al*. (1979), in a factor-analytic study, demonstrated, with two separate groups of subjects, that for the variables concerned, three factors emerged. These were labelled integrative motivation, foreign language achievement and anxiety, respectively. However, what is interesting is that the anxiety tests did not load appreciably on the achievement factor, implying that while the construct of anxiety may be important in describing people, it may not always be implicated in language learning.

In marked contrast to the questionnaire-based investigations of anxiety, there have also been attempts to record more subjective reactions through the use of diaries. Bailey (1983), in a review of such studies, finds many examples of the importance of anxiety, and its effect on learning behaviours. She also reports individual differences in the tendency to experience anxiety (presumably trait anxiety). Interestingly, with many learners, herself included, anxiety becomes more important because of the related trait of competitiveness, which is often the driving force for worry. The insights from diary studies, the information on the sources of anxiety, discussed earlier, and the moderating influences of competitiveness (which is bad), and solidarity and inter-student friendship (which is good) could be a useful basis for teacher intervention to channel student anxiety more effectively.

Two broad conclusions now seem warranted about anxiety research. First, there does seem to be a relationship between measures of anxiety and learning, but it is rather weak, with most studies suggesting a negative correlation of about –0.30. Further, additional variables such as age, ability, stage of learning, proficiency level, learner competitiveness, and class solidarity and friendship may all affect the basic relationship. Additional and more complex designs are needed to tease out the different contributions of these potentially important variables. Second, anxiety research has been rather narrow in scope. In terms of setting, there tends to be a concentration on classroom-based research in an EFL context, mainly with secondary school and adult learners. There has been relatively little research in ESL settings and with learners under the age of 10. In addition, there has been little attempt to look for interactions, for condition-seeking effects (discussed more extensively in the next chapter) to build up a picture of where anxiety is likely to be most potent in its effects, e.g. with low-ability students in intensive courses followed by examinations. There has also been an over-reliance on questionnaire scale approaches. It would be desirable to have alternative types of measure available such as observer ratings or introspective evidence. Indeed, there might be potential in using a more ethnographic perspective altogether, following Bailey (1983), to gain a clear understanding of such issues as the role of 'face' in the development of anxiety. In any case, more extended methodologies, settings and goals with anxiety research might enable us to step outside the rather restrictive framework within which such studies are presently conducted.

7

Interactions

The last four chapters have taken a straightforward approach to ID research, surveying relatively circumscribed areas such as aptitude and learner strategies. In each, there have been substantial findings to report, and established research methodologies. The situation is rather different in the current chapter. Here we are concerned with the conditional effects of a particular type of treatment (e.g. methodology) on particular types of learner (e.g. high vs. low aptitude). We are looking, that is, at Aptitude–Treatment Interaction (ATI), or, as it has also been called, condition-seeking research (McLaughlin 1987). Because there are fewer findings, and there is less agreement on research methodology, it will be useful, initially, to look at a wider framework for research into language learning, since this will allow us more easily to see what research *might* be done, and how existing methodologies and results fit in.

A framework for research on language learning

In Chapter 1 a simple taxonomic model was proposed, taken from Naiman *et al.* (1978). A revised version of this model is presented in Figure 7.1. There are two main changes compared to the model presented earlier. First of all, a new box has been added, *Opportunities for TL Use*, to reflect the growing importance attached to communicative approaches and a 'talking to learn' perspective. This box is influenced, independently, by the social context *and* classroom and materials. In addition, it should be noted that classrooms and materials are postulated as having a direct effect upon learning.

The second change is in the Classrooms and Materials box. The box still contains headings such as syllabus, methodology, materials and

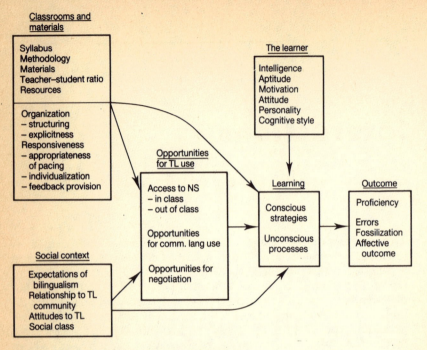

Figure 7.1: Influences on language learning

teacher–student ratio. In addition, though, there is a section on more organizational and 'efficiency' issues, such as the degree of structuring and explicitness, and the responsiveness of the teacher to the individual student. The first set of factors here, e.g. syllabus, etc. are more concerned with issues specific to language teaching while the second set derive more from general pedagogic principle and practice. The language-related aspects of classrooms can only be part of the Classrooms and Materials box for two reasons. First, despite the energy such factors have generated, comparative studies of e.g. methodology, have been remarkably inconclusive. Second, we are only now beginning to devise adequate observational instruments to address the functioning of these factors (e.g. Mitchell *et al*. 1981, Allen *et al*. 1984). The problem we have, therefore, is that to investigate aptitude–treatment interactions we need some system of categories for classrooms which represent our best guess of what constitutes the 'treatment'. Paradoxically, the most useful research into successful language teaching practices seems to have derived from influences other than *language* teaching, and to be more concerned with notions of the 'efficiency' of instruction. As Richards and Rodgers (ms) put it:

Researchers who have studied the behaviours of effective teachers begin with the assumption that teachers work in ways that are to an extent independent of both methods and curricula (e.g. Good 1979, Green 1982, Tikunoff 1985) and that the characteristics of effective teaching can be determined quite apart from the nominal method which the teacher may be thought to be following. (p. 13)

Basically, such studies, e.g. Tikonoff (1985), have demonstrated that efficient teachers have better classroom management skills, and run classrooms where a high proportion of learners spend a high proportion of the time concentrating on the task at hand. Wong-Fillmore (1985) suggests that successful classes (in bilingual education) have formal lessons with clear boundaries; predictable lesson structure; built-in repetition and routinized language; clear and fair turn-allocation; and teachers responsive to differing individual needs of individual students. These research findings, have, then, been reflected in the changes in the Classrooms and Materials box.

This analysis of the classroom now allows us to return to Figure 7.1, and to the headings for the four major boxes of independent variables its contains: (a) classrooms and materials, (b) social context, (c) opportunities for TL use, and (d) the learner. In principle, the last of these groups, the learner, could enter into interactions with each of the other categories. We have seen some indications of this in earlier chapters, e.g. Kruidenier and Clement's (1986) work, which argues for an interaction between motivational orientation and opportunities for target language use. Any complete analysis will need to consider all potential interactions of this sort. However, the main thrust of this chapter will be on potential interactions between the learner and instructional conditions, i.e. with the Classrooms and Materials box. We will examine such instructional conditions in terms of four major sub-categories relative to Figure 7.1. These are *Language Teaching Principles*, which comprises syllabus, methodology and materials; *Resources*, which includes the teacher–student ratio, the amount of money available, the existence of specialist resources such as audio-visual equipment, language laboratories and CALL; *Classroom Organization*, which subsumes the degree of structuring of teaching, the explicitness of instruction, and the participant organization of the classroom; and *Responsiveness*, which concerns the appropriateness of pacing, the degree of individualization, and the amount and nature of feedback provision. Further, we will make the traditional distinction in the Learner box between cognitive variables (intelligence, aptitude and cognitive style), and affective variables (motivation, attitude and personality). This new focus is shown in Figure 7.2.

We now have four classroom and two learner categories, at a crude

CLASSROOMS

Language teaching principles
– syllabus
– methodology
– materials

Resources
– teacher–student ratio
– money available
– specialist resource
  availability

Classroom organization
– degree of structuring
– instructional explicitness
– participant organization

Responsiveness
– appropriateness of pacing
– individualization
– feedback provision

LEARNERS

Cognitive abilities
– intelligence
– language aptitude
– cognitive style

Affective factors
– motivation and attitude
– personality

Figure 7.2: The learner and classroom boxes

level, and twelve classroom and five learner groups at a more delicate
level, implying *sixty* potential interactions. Quite clearly, all these
potential interactions are not of equal importance: the point of a
representation such as Figure 7.2 is to show what the possibilities are, so
that one can then start to assess research priorities. In the following
sections, therefore, we will cover the research which has been
completed under the headings of first cognitive, and then affective
learner factors. Then we come back to Figure 7.2 at the end of the
chapter to assess where we now stand with condition-seeking research,
and what still remains to be done.

Aptitude–treatment interaction: cognitive influences

A few studies have examined possible interactions between instructional features and learner *cognitive* characteristics. Seven studies of
this type are shown in Table 7.1, where they are categorized in terms of
(a) the material to be learned, (b) the instructional feature being
manipulated, and (c) the relevant learner characteristics.

Carroll and Spearritt (1967) (cited in Cronbach and Snow 1977)
studied a large group of 12-year-old children taught via an instruction
booklet. Some children received instruction on the rules of grammar,
one rule at a time, with the rules being presented in ordered fashion, and

Table 7.1: Interaction studies with cognitive learner variables

Researchers	Learning material	Instructional contrast	Learner variable
Carroll and Spearritt	Artifical language	Ordered and isolated rule presentation + error explanation	IQ
Nation and McLaughlin	Artifical language	Explicit vs. implicit	Expert vs. Novice
Gallegos	Passive	Self-pacing vs. slow external pacing	IQ
Maier and Jacobs	General instructional programme	Ordered small steps vs. Scrambled Order	IQ
Zampogna *et al.*	General programme	Individualized vs. conventional	Cognitive development
Abraham	Participle structures	Inductive vs. deductive	Field (in)-dependence
Wesche	General programme	Grammar vs. situational	Analytic vs. memory based

with errors being explained. The other group were presented with several rules at once, in a random manner, and for them, errors were not explained. Achievement, measured by how long it took to work through the instructional booklet, was significantly related to IQ in the systematic presentation/error-feedback group, whereas other students (presumably the non-high IQ) did better on the less systematically presented/no error-feedback form of instruction.

The other study involving the learning of an artificial language, i.e. a miniature language system involving letter sequences, was by Nation and McLaughlin (1986). Two forms of instruction were used. Under implicit learning conditions learners were presented with exemplars of linguistic rules (without being told there was a rule to be learned, simply to pay close attention to the stimuli). In fact there were two sub-groups under the implicit learning condition. The first were presented the 20 stimuli in a structured order, while the second were presented with a random ordering. Then subjects were then told that the stimuli they had seen had followed a rule for letter order, and were tested with 100 new stimuli (50 different exemplars, each presented twice, consisting of 25 'grammatical' and 25 'ungrammatical' strings). In the explicit learning condition, students were told at the outset that there would be rules to learn which governed the letter-order of the strings they would be presented. Once again, there were two orderings: systematic and

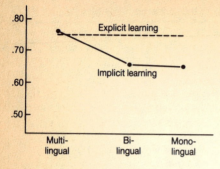

Figure 7.3: Effects of subject background on letter rule learning

random. Subject groups were either monolingual, bilingual, or multi-lingual. Nation and McLaughlin (1986) used these previous learning experiences to contrast 'novice' (mono and bilingual) learners with 'experts' (multilinguals).

There were significant differences (not discussed here) for structured vs. random presentation for both learning conditions, i.e. structured presentations led to (slightly) more effective learning, but no inter-actions with subject groups, i.e. neither the 'experts' nor the 'novices' did better or worse with structured or random presentation. The results for the implicit vs. explicit comparison are shown in Figure 7.3. There was a strong main effect for learning condition (p < .001) and also for subject group (p < .001) as shown in Figure 7.3. Explicit learning led to greater success, as regards learning condition, and multilingual subjects performed best, as regards subject group. Most important for the present discussion, there was an interaction between learning condition and subject groups (p < .01). As Figure 7.3 shows, for the monolingual and bilingual groups (the 'novices') the learning condition, explicit or implicit, made a significant difference. In contrast, for the multilingual subjects, the 'experts', there was little difference in achievement between the two learning conditions. One interpretation of this would be that such learners are able to cope with informal learning environ-ments, and make sense of them, an interpretation consistent with the discussion of the role of aptitude in informal settings given in Chapter 3. As Nation and McLaughlin put it:

> This finding suggests that the superiority of 'the good language learner' over other subjects with less experience in language learning may derive, at least in part, from an ability to abstract structural information from linguistic stimuli under conditions where subjects are simply exposed to exemplars with no instruc-

tions to learn the material or derive underlying rules. (Nation and McLaughlin 1986, p. 51)

There are two studies which focus on isolated grammar points. Gallegos (1968) looked at the passive voice in Spanish with 110 high school students. The instruction was via tape recordings, and the task variation contrasted three tape versions – slow, fast or self-paced. There was a trend (non-significant) for high IQ students to do better with self-pacing, and for low IQ students to do better with slow, external pacing.

The other limited-grammar focus study, in this case on participle constructions, is by Abraham (1985). She contrasted inductive and deductive teaching, all of which was computer-based. In the *inductive approach*, many examples of participle phrases in context were provided, active and passive forms, and derived from relative and adverbial clauses. There was some structuring of presentation, in that the passive forms were presented first 'since their formation is more straightforward'. Error-feedback provided hints for correcting the response, up to three attempts, after which the correct form was supplied. The *deductive approach* contained an introduction on participle phrases, followed by instructions on the derivation of such phrases from relative or adverbial clauses, and on passive compared to active participial phrases. Eight example sentences were presented, followed by 22 practice sentences (with error-feedback, as for the inductive learning).

Subjects were classified in terms of field (in)dependence by means of the Group Embedded Figures Test ((GEFT): Witkin *et al*. 1971). Abraham (1985) reports that although there was no evidence that lesson type had any significant main effect, there was an interaction, as indicated by the slope of the regression line, between field-(in)dependence and lesson type. Field-independent subjects performed better with the deductive lesson while field-dependent subjects performed better with the inductive (example) lesson. However, not a great deal of the variance on the post-test scores was accounted for by field-independence, suggesting that, consistent with the discussion in Chapter 6, this construct has, at best, a slight effect on performance.

So far the research we have examined has tried to set up controlled, brief studies. We come now to some longer-term studies. Maier and Jacobs (1966) looked at achievement in a Spanish course on quite a large scale and over a one-year period. Seventeen classes were given instruction by means of a programme with small steps and ordered material, while 22 other classes were presented with a 'scrambled' programme in which the material did not progress in an orderly fashion. Overall achievement in each programme, perhaps surprisingly, did not differ, but there was a trend for classes with higher IQ students to do better on the scrambled course, and for classes with lower IQ students to do better on the ordered version, a contrast with the Carroll and Spearritt study mentioned earlier.

Zampogna, Gentile, Papalia and Gordon (1976) contrasted two types of instructional programme – one in which there was individualized instruction, and a second which was more conventionally lockstep in organization. They found that a higher level of cognitive development was associated with greater achievement in the individualized programme, but not in the more conventional programme.

Finally, we have a study by Wesche (1981), mentioned already in Chapter 3, examining the relationship between instructional methodology and aptitude type. Three groups of learner were identified. An analytic group consisted of learners whose MLAT was not below the 40th percentile but whose Part IV, Words in Sentences, score was above the 60th percentile, and who, in interview, demonstrated facility with analytical tasks. Phonetic coding, memory and auditory ability were not used in assigning students to this group. The memory/auditory learning group consisted of students with below-average analytic abilities but higher auditory and memory abilities. Finally, the remaining students were assigned to various levels of the core group, i.e. all those students who had fairly flat aptitude profiles.

There were also three different instructional approaches. In the analytic approach:

> grammatical explanations provide an advance conceptual framework before the material is presented, and every attempt is made to assure that new learning is meaningful.

In the functional approach:

> new material is organized around specific situations and language uses rather than according to a strict progression of linguistic structures. Emphasis is on language use in interpersonal situations . . . with as many contextual cues as possible. (Wesche 1981, p. 128)

Finally, the core course, the Audio-Visual Method, is *Dialogue Canada*, in which dialogues are memorized which accompany and are illustrated by slides. Oral structure drills then build upon the material introduced in the memorized dialogues. In this method:

> This inductive, 'global' approach requires the student to work by 'successive approximation', since the oral stimuli used are generally too complex to allow more than partial assimilation on first presentation. The student gradually completes and perfects the response with repeated exposure to the same stimuli. Explicit grammatical explanation, translation, and the use of reading and

writing in the early phase of training are seldom permitted.'
(Wesche 1981, p. 127)

The research examining interaction effects was in two parts. In the
first part, the Analytic and Audio-Visual groups were investigated
when matched with an 'appropriate' method, i.e. all students were
matched. It was reported that, under these circumstances, a high level
of both teacher and student satisfaction was expressed, and that there
was no significant difference in achievement between the groups,
suggesting that alternative routes to the same level of achievement is a
realistic goal.

More interestingly, in another study, groups of analytic students
were placed half in the Analytic method, and half in the Audio-Visual
method, i.e. half the students were deliberately *mismatched* with a non-
analytic method. The results of this study are shown in Table 7.2. The
first three measures here concern affective reactions by the students. It
can be seen that the matched students have greater interest in foreign
languages; a more positive general attitude towards the method; and
lower anxiety. Of the four achievement scores, three are significant in
favour of the matched students, and one is non-significant, with all of
the significances at the 0.01 level. Equally interestingly, where the
achievement scores attain significance, the standard deviation of the
matched group is noticeably smaller than that for the unmatched
group. Matching students with method may result in more homogeneous achievement, as the whole group moves together, while the
mismatched group seems to contain a wider spread of achievement,
suggesting that some students have coped well with the inappropriate

Table 7.2: Matching of analytic students with method types

Variable	Approach	N	Max	Mean	SD	T-Value
Interest in foreign languages	A-V	88	6	4.4	1.0	− 6.4**
	Analytical			5.2	0.6	
General attitude to method	A-V	26	6	3.58	1.4	− 2.17*
	Analytical			4.03	0.9	
French class anxiety	A-V	92	6	2.9	1.1	− 2.48*
	Analytical			2.6	1.1	
Achievement test 730: Listening	A-V	46	32	21.5	5.1	− 4.40**
	Analytical			25.3	3.5	
Achievement test 730: Oral	A-V	46	75	56.4	10	.65 (ns)
	Analytical			55.0	10.5	
Achievement test 745: Listening	A-V	43	21	13.8	3.9	− 2.9**
	Analytical			16.0	3.0	
Achievement test 745: Oral	A-V	43	42	31.4	7.2	− 3.73**
	Analytical			35.8	3.5	

methodology, and have perhaps a wider repertoire of learning capacities, but that others have been disadvantaged.

The studies reviewed in this section have not been numerous, but the results are interesting. We certainly need to look for some generalizations from the existing findings. For example, one group of studies has examined the relationship between IQ and some aspect of instructional presentation. Here the studies by Gallegos (1968) and Zampogna *et al.* (1976) suggest that IQ is positively related to performance *where the individual can exert control over rate of learning*. To put this another way, it could well be that higher-level students become bored with slow or conventional instruction. They succeed when engaged, but do not when turned off by the slowness of the materials.

The second group of studies is more difficult to generalize about, since there are discrepancies in the findings. Maier and Jacobs (1966) found IQ to be positively related to scrambled (as opposed to small-step) instruction, while Carroll and Spearritt (1967) reported that IQ was positively related to ordered presentation of material (as opposed to random). Nation and McLaughlin (1986), finally, reported expert learners to perform equally well under explicit and implicit instruction, as though their expertise allowed them to impose their own structure on the data to be learned, consistent with Maier and Jacob's (1966) finding. Further research is needed to try and account for these discrepancies. It seems likely that additional, uncontrolled variables underlie the apparent contradictions. Table 7.3 makes this a little

Table 7.3: Parameters from the three studies

Researchers	Material	Length	Comparisons	Result
Carroll and Spearritt	Artificial language	60 page	(a) Ordered vs unordered rules (b) Isolated rules vs simultaneous rules (c) Error feedback vs no feedback	IQ related to ordered isolated, feedback condition
Maier and Jacobs	General instruction		(a) Small vs. large steps (b) Ordered vs scrambled programme	IQ related to scrambled, large step programme
Nation and McLaughlin	Artificial language	2 experiments	(a) Implicit vs explicit (b) Ordered vs disordered presentation	'Experts' not affected by implicit learning condition

clearer since it illustrates some of the variable manipulations which were not the same in the different studies.

The problem is similar to trying to solve three simultaneous equations with five unknowns! There are too many possible explanations. There is some evidence that more talented learners (if this term can be used to cover IQ and multilingual subjects) are able to cope with less structured or even confusing material, and even possibly thrive on it. Such an interpretation, consistent with the arguments for the importance of aptitude in informal learning situations, would also imply that structured presentations would have the laudable effect of 'equalizing out' the IDs which produce differences in achievement in less helpful circumstances, i.e. instruction is particularly effective with weaker learners. Alternatively, one might argue, from the Carroll and Spearritt study, that IQ enables learners to exploit the structure that is provided for them to the full, although it is noteworthy that Nation and McLaughlin's (1986) ordering vs. random condition did not produce any effect, main or interaction, with their various subject groups.

Basically, we have too many possible explanations because additional comparisons were built in to each study. Possibly IQ does profit from unordered rule presentation and the conflicting Carroll and Spearritt (1967) result is explained because error-feedback interacts even more strongly with IQ. Since there are no studies investigating the effects of feedback on different types of learner, we simply cannot say. Alternatively, we could interpret the various findings through 'rate of presentation' effects, or, an aspect of this issue, the amount of challenge in the materials. It could well be that the degree of engagement of the learner with the materials is the critical factor. Where lockstep, slow presentation operates, quicker learners may be turned off, whereas more challenging material may actually stimulate them. It could be, that is, that IQ was related to the 'scrambled' programme in Maier and Jacobs (1966) because it also involved large steps, and therefore a potentially faster rate of progress. With the Carroll and Spearritt (1967) instructional booklet, IQ may have been related to the ordered presentation of rules because learners could progress along this structured order at whatever speed, however rapid, they felt capable of. This interpretation would be consistent with the results from Gallegos (1968) and Zampogna *et al.* (1976), presented above. Further research is needed to resolve these issues.

Aptitude–treatment interactions: affective/interpersonal influences

When we turn to potential interactions between affective variables and classroom organization, we see clearer connections with more contemporary language teaching methods. Sato (1982), for example, investigated the relationship between wait-time and student response. She found that increasing the wait period allowed by the teacher between some eliciting move, e.g. a cue in a drill, or a question, could have a considerable influence on the participation and responsiveness of different students. Some students, that is, seemed prepared to respond after quite brief wait-times, while others preferred to allow a longer interval to elapse before responding. Most important, if the teacher did not allow a sufficiently long wait-time, such students simply did not respond. In relation to aptitude–treatment interactions, Sato (1983) reports that Hispanic students seemed to require briefer wait-times, and seemed to be ready to respond to teacher soliciting moves quite quickly. Asian background students, often Japanese, in contrast, seemed to want to allow an adequately reverential silent period to elapse before responding. The implication of this study for the amount of interaction engaged in by the different types of learner is clear, especially since willingness to respond appropriately to whatever wait-times are being 'offered' could have a considerable multiplicative effect on additional and more extended interaction opportunities.

A number of interaction studies have been conducted under the direction of Wong-Fillmore (1982, 1986) who has been concerned with the relationship between various classroom participant structures and learner individual differences. The structure of the classrooms has been analysed around two variables. The first is simply the proportion of NS children to NNS children. The second variable concerns the nature of the classroom organization. Wong-Fillmore (1982) first describes classrooms which have an open organization, where the teacher is not dominant, and where much of the activity is group and project based. In such classrooms there is considerable scope for children to interact with other children, and to use language with them. Wong-Fillmore (1982) contrasts such open, group-oriented classrooms with others which are much more teacher-dominated. In these most of the activities are teacher-led, indeed teacher-dominated, with much less scope for children to interact with one another. These two modes of classroom organization have implications for the roles that learners can have. Wong-Fillmore focuses, first of all, on the proportions of NS to NNS children in the various classes. She presents the following cross-tabulation (Table 7.4) of NS/NNS proportions and classroom organization in four different classrooms.

There is quite a range here, from 34 per cent in Class 1, to 92 per cent in Class 4. The simple-minded prediction one would make in this case is that the ranking of the classes, 1 to 4, on the NS/NNS ratio would also be the ranking of the favourableness of the differing environments for the NNS. The higher the proportion of NS children, the greater the inevitability of interaction, and the greater the force for language

Table 7.4: Proportions of NNS children by classroom organization

Classroom organization	Student composition Mixed NES/LES/Eng speaking	High NES
Open	Class 1: 34%	Class 3: 79%
Teacher directed	Class 2: 48%	Class 4: 92%

Figures are the percentage of Non-English speaking children (NES) and Limited English speaking (LES)

Table 7.5: Indices of improvement with NES speakers

	Raw numbers Begin of yr	End of yr	Difference	Percentage of NES who learned no English
Class 1	14	2	− 12	14
Class 2	15	6	− 9	40
Class 3	18	7	− 11	39
Class 4	14	0	− 14	0

development through the need to communicate meanings. In fact, however, the results did not follow this straightforward prediction. If one compares the data on NES at the beginning and end of the school year a different, and more complex picture emerges, as shown in Table 7.5. The most impressive figures are those for Classes 1 and 4, the maximally different classes. We have, in other words, a clear example of an interaction cross-over effect, as graphing the above data, in Figure 7.4, illustrates.

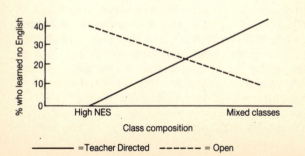

Figure 7.4: The interaction between group composition and classroom organization

If we try to account for this interaction, some additional information about class composition is relevant. Classes 1 and 2 were Spanish bilingual, Class 3 an English programme (with a Cantonese assistant, reflecting the ethnic background of many of the participants), and Class 4 was Cantonese bilingual. Wong-Fillmore (1982) contrasts the differing expectations of the two ethnic groups as follows:

> There seem to be striking differences among children according to whether they are inclined to orient their activities in the classroom towards adults or peers. On this matter, there appear to fairly marked group differences; the Chinese children we observed tended generally to be more concerned with the expectations and opinions of the adults of their world than they were with those of their classmates. They appeared to look much more consistently to their teachers and to the other adults in the classroom (such as members of the resident research team) for guidance and support than they did to one another. By contrast, the Spanish speaking children in our study appeared far more attuned to their peers than they were to adults. While they obviously liked being around their teachers, they seemed to turn more to peers for ideas and directions than they did to their teachers. (Wong Fillmore 1982, p. 166)

What we seem to have, therefore, are two classes with combinations of favourable conditions, and two with much less favourable situations. One of the effective classes (Class 1) has an open mode of organization (permitting and encouraging contact between children), a favourable mixture of NS-NNS children (66 per cent NS: 34 per cent NNS), and an orientation towards group work on the part of the children (Spanish). The consequence, despite what is reported as an enormous class of 53 children, is relatively few children at the end of the year with no English. Interaction seems to have produced language development with children who were keen to interact. The other successful class contained a teacher-directed organization (with children looking to the teacher for leadership and guidance, and not to one another), a poor NS/NNS ratio (8 per cent NS: 92 per cent NNS); and children whose expectations about educational arrangements were that they would look to the teacher to transmit information to them (Chinese). And this combination was also effective, moving from 14 children at the beginning of the year with no English, to none at the end. In this case, it seems to have been instruction, or at least teacher-led activity, which produced language development in children keen to accept the teacher-based norms.

The other two classes were less successful (although it should be noted that less successful does not mean completely unsuccessful, as Table 7.5 shows). In any case, Class 2 had the combination of teacher-direction; a good NS/NNS split (52 : 48); but children who were group-oriented (Spanish). It would seem that the multiple opportunities for interaction afforded by the presence of NS children was not enough in itself, and that classroom organization frustrated children from exploiting *some* of the conditions for collaborative learning. One wonders if the results would have been even worse if there had been teacher direction with these same children but with a less favourable NS/NNS mix. Finally, Class 3 brings together an open class, a relatively small percentage of NS (21 : 79), and children oriented towards a teacher. The children, that is, would not be expected to interact, on a group basis, with NS children even if they were there, and were presumably disconcerted by a teacher who was non-directive and group-oriented.

The Berkeley research is both fascinatingly suggestive, and simultaneously difficult to evaluate. The fascination derives from the way interaction is shown to be relative to classroom organization, learner type and interaction style. One wonders whether similar condition-seeking frameworks would yield greater dividends for traits such as extroversion, anxiety and risk-taking, which the last chapter concluded were only weakly related, at best, to success: possibly more subtle research designs would produce different results.

But there are also problems with any interpretation of the research. Most serious is the lack of substantial quantification. In some ways this might be considered to be an unfair criticism. A great deal of the value of the Berkeley research derives from the ethnographic approach taken, especially when it captures the classroom orientations and preferences of the children concerned. But one would also like more detail on the nature of the programme concerned; on what it means to be an open or teacher-directed classroom. Above all, one would like to have a clear picture of the proficiency levels attained by the children. Wong-Fillmore (1982), for example, distinguishes between LES (Limited English Speaking) and NES (No English Speaking) children, with both groups present in all classrooms. The crucial issue is what the terms LES and NES mean. How much English do you need to move from being NES to LES? Further, it would be helpful if there were overall indices of improvement which tell us more than '14 NES children moved out of this category during the year'. Did they just scrape out of this bottom-rung level, or did they make substantial progress?

Finally, there is the issue of the confounding of variables. Table 7.4 shows that Classes 1 and 2 (the Spanish bilingual classes) contained relatively high proportions of English speaking children (66 per cent and 52 per cent respectively), whereas Classes 3 and 4 contained much lower proportions (21 per cent and 8 per cent). One wonders, therefore, whether the results obtained were due to the NS/NNS ratios of the first two groups or to the ethnic background (with the implications this latter might have for preferred classroom participation structure). To test out these differences one would need to have a research design of larger scale, with a greater range of NS/NNS children in (say) four Spanish background groups, and similarly with classes of Chinese children. Then we would be able to see more clearly how Spanish children would do in teacher-led groups with few NS children, or whether Chinese children could cope perfectly well with open classrooms if there are a lot of native speakers. This would resolve the issue of whether the causal variables are educational (NS/NNS ratios) or ID (cultural or personality based).

Conclusions: interaction studies

The three major conclusions we can draw from this chapter are first, that the completed condition-seeking research has been some of the most fascinating in applied linguistics; second, that there are many studies whose interpretation is not clear for research-design reasons; and third, that abysmally little research of this sort has actually been done. As regards the first conclusion, almost any language teacher will voice the belief that it is the appropriate combination of instructional conditions matched with the appropriate learners that produces success. The research reported in this chapter is mostly consistent with this viewpoint. When researchers have gone looking for interactions, they have frequently found them. The era of looking for across-the-board solutions, whether with syllabus, methodology, or any other aspect of instruction, should draw to a close, or at least be reduced considerably in importance, to be replaced by condition-seeking studies.

The second conclusion concerns the inadequacies of the research designs that have been used so far. It is clear that many variables may influence results, and they may do so in different directions. Consequently, it is important for investigators to design studies very carefully. In the cognitive area we saw an example of this when it was difficult to interpret the role of IQ interacting with random or ordered presentation of materials because the degree of challenge in the materials may have been confounded with mode and rate of presentation. So it is important to control as many relevant variables as possible. In the affective area, we also saw in the Berkeley research, (Wong-Fillmore 1982), a confounding of NS/NNS ratio and classroom orientation of different groups of learners. As a result, interpretation of results has to be done circumspectly.

Finally, in relation to the third conclusion, we need to make the connection again with the framework outlined at the beginning of the chapter in Figure 7.2 to try and stand back and relate completed ATI research to what might be done. When we do this, the most striking result is to find how the existing ATI studies have, with one exception, focused on the Classroom Organization and Responsiveness areas. There has been no condition-seeking research on the effects of Resources (though see Chappelle and Jamieson 1986 for some speculation). There has been only one study (Wesche 1981) examining one limited aspect of methodology related to learner type, i.e. nothing at all on syllabus or materials or mode of presentation. Further, although the majority of ATI studies have concentrated on features located in the Classroom Organization and Responsiveness boxes, i.e. efficiency of instruction variables, one can hardly say that these areas have been exhaustively covered. Only limited features of structuring, explicitness, participant organization, pacing and individualization have been investigated. In addition, most of the studies have used unrealistic materials and instructional conditions, leaving considerable problems of external validity. This does not mean that such studies are not important or useful, simply that they need to be supplemented by alternative approaches. Further, there has been no research at all (unless one counts this aspect of the Carroll and Spearritt (1967) study) on feedback provision, i.e. the possibility that different learner types respond differentially to different types of feedback provision. So, quite clearly, there is enormous scope for additional ATI research.

But it is also worth considering some of the additional components of the model shown in Figure 7.1. There is considerable scope for interactional studies involving acquisitional processes. It would be interesting to see, for example, if different learner types relied to different extents on various acquisitional processes, especially if this were linked to different types of instructional materials and different types of exposure to the target language. It is also vital to broaden the nature of the criterion measures used. Almost all the condition-seeking studies conducted so far have relied upon language-like measures, often of an extremely artificial nature, as the criterion performance to be accounted for. It is important to consider more naturalistic and communicative performance if not only to reflect current views of language teaching. This might radically change our ideas on the sort of interaction effects that are important. Similarly, the Social Context and Opportunities for TL Use boxes could also be the basis for condition-seeking studies, with IDs such as personality, risk-taking, motivation patterns, etc. all influencing the type and number of interactions that learners engage in.

8

Conclusions and implications

The final chapter will be in three sections. The first will summarize the main content of the book, and so condense the argument and evidence. The second will consider the role of theory in ID research. This was touched on in Chapter 1 but will be developed more fully here, and it will be argued that a concatenated view of theory is most appropriate for current ID work. The third section will outline the sort of research which could now be most usefully be done within an ID framework.

Generalizations from individual difference studies

1: Some people are endowed with better cognitive/linguistic abilities for language learning than others

(Chapter 3): This generalization is simply that people vary in their language aptitude, and that such variation has considerable significance for language learning success. This claim is justified principally by the accumulation of studies demonstrating a positive (and generally substantial) relationship between measure of aptitude and measures of achievement, where correlations of the order of 0.40 to 0.60 are fairly standard. An important part of the justification is the robustness of such results, particularly when compared to those found between other ID traits and achievement. Another part of the justification derives from the theoretical discussions of aptitude (Carroll 1981, Skehan 1986a) which attempt to relate aptitude to the processing skills involved in language learning. The point should also be made that while the relevance of aptitude for formal learning situations has been demonstrated, the evidence is less impressive for a connection with success in informal settings. For such a claim only the evidence from Reves (1983) exists at present.

2: Aptitude is multi-componential: (a) people can have strengths and weaknesses, and (b) learner types exist
(Chapter 3): We saw in Chapter 3 that there are (fairly) independent components of aptitude. Three were highlighted; a language analytic capacity; memory ability; and phonemic coding ability. This implies that two people with the same overall aptitude score may have different component abilities. The pedagogic implication is that instructional efficiency could be improved by taking these strengths and weaknesses into account, and designing instruction accordingly. A development of the multi-component view of aptitude proposes that there are learner types – characteristic preferences in information processing, with some learners leaning more towards an analytic view of language, with others working more naturally from a memory orientation.

3: Language Analytic IDs in second language learning have connections with similar IDs in first language learning
(Chapter 3): Even though most first language investigators focus on universal processes, Wells (1985, 1986) has shown that massive IDs exist in *rate* of first language acquisition. Follow up research has now shown (Skehan 1986c; Skehan 1988) that there are clear connections between syntactic aspects of first language development and the language analytic aspects of foreign language aptitude. Those children whose syntactic development is most rapid tend to be those children with higher foreign language aptitude. The implication is that a capacity to process syntactic information does not completely atrophy with age, nor is it overlaid without trace by other aspects of cognitive development. For some, that is, processing linguistic material comes with greater facility than for others.

4: People vary in their adjustment to decontextualized learning situations (e.g. education)
(Chapter 3): The follow-up to the Bristol Project (especially Skehan 1986c, in press) as well as some of the main findings from the Bristol Project (Wells 1985) suggested that children (and presumably adults) vary considerably in their capacity to profit from instruction when this instruction is context-disembedded, i.e. not directly arising out of real and familiar experiences. With language study this implies that some children will be more able to see the relevance and generality of language teaching formats which emphasize language as a subject of study, rather than as a means of natural communication.

5: Learning orientations influence motivational patterns, and therefore language learning success
(Chapter 4): Gardner (1985) has established that motivational orientations are important for language study. However, the original

distinction between integrative and instrumental orientations is less prominent. It is clear that there are additional orientations (as Kruidenier and Clement (1986) have demonstrated) which complicate the issue, not least when we examine interactions between orientations and learning contexts (e.g. minority vs. majority language settings).

6: The direction of causation in motivation studies is unclear
(Chapter 4): Clearly Gardner's position is that orientation, and then motivation, are causal variables, and achievement in language study is the caused, dependent variable. This view has been challenged by Hermann (1980) and Strong (1984) who both argue that the direction of causation should be reversed – success and achievement (however achieved) in turn cause motivation. Certainly, as Chapter 4 showed, one should not study motivation in isolation from other aspects of the learning situation, and one needs to take into account the motivating agents working on the learner (e.g. teacher, materials, examinations, etc.) to get a fuller picture *within which* motivational orientation may play a part. But above all here, one needs further research of a longitudinal and ethnomethodological nature. Rather than be dependent on influences from test data, that is, we need to monitor changes in motivational levels over time which are linked to external events and influences. Only this will enable us to sort out patterns of causation unequivocally.

7: The variability of motivational orientations in different learning situations requires further study
(Chapter 4): Kruidenier and Clement (1986) have shown that progress can be made in establishing systematic correspondences between motivational orientation and learning setting. This confirms and extends earlier research such as Gardner and Lambert's (1972) in the Philippines, and Lukmani's (1972) in India which described settings where instrumental motivation was more important than integrative. What we may need here (and elsewhere!) is a theory of *situations* into which hypotheses about motivational orientations can then fit more meaningfully.

8: Language learners use a variety of strategies
(Chapter 5): There is now considerable evidence from self-report and observational studies that learners use a variety of strategies. There is less agreement, however, between different investigators, on what these strategies are, or, more importantly, how the findings of one investigator can be related to those of another. Nor is there any agreement on the way in which strategy data can be collected. Certainly attempts to

capitalize on self-report data as the basis for the production of more objective and questionnaire-based methods have not been successful.

9: The most useful classification of strategies at present is between metacognitive/cognitive/and social strategies

(Chapter 5): O'Malley *et al.* (1985a) have proposed this threefold division. Metacognitive strategies function as higher-order and more general strategies which are more pervasive and organizational in influence. They serve to give direction to other strategies. Cognitive strategies, in contrast, concern more specific behaviours which are themselves linked to more circumscribed learning situations. In some ways this is a strength, and in others, a weakness, since it involves a lack of transferability. Finally, social strategies are not very well developed in the O'Malley *et al.* (1985a) model. There is considerable scope for expansion in this area, to incorporate more completely some of the insights from Naiman *et al.* (1978); to enable the role of strategies when interaction with NS is a potential part of learning to be incorporated; and to extend the model to enable some coverage of informal learning situations. With these expansions, the tripartite division could bring considerable systematicity to future strategy research.

10: Metacognitive strategies could well link up with aptitude factors involving decontextualized learning

(Chapters 3 and 5): There is a striking resemblance between the sorts of capacities which underlie metacognitive strategies, on the one hand, and aspects of what are measured by language aptitude tests (cf. the decontextualization component) on the other. It could well be that similar abilities have been focused on by both sets of investigators, working from two different research traditions. In each case the relevant ID concern a capacity to stand back, reflect upon, plan and organize one's experience.

11: Current evidence on the trainability of learning strategies is not encouraging

(Chapter 5): One of the main motives for the study of strategies is the hope that they are causative and that they can be trained. Discovering what the most effective strategies are, that is, might allow them to be taught to less successful learners, thus enabling these learners to progress more quickly. This belief underlies recent work such as that of Ellis and Sinclair (1987). Unfortunately, the current evidence on the trainability of strategies is not encouraging. The effects that have been found (Hassall 1984; O'Malley *et al.* 1985b) tend to have been very slight, so that one cannot really speak of the efficiency of learning being transformed. However, the study of strategies is very much in its early days. It would be premature to discount the possibility of effective training in the future.

12: There is considerable scope for connections between ID research and individualized instruction

The 1970s and 1980s have been a period during which 'the learner' has been, rather belatedly, brought to centre stage. One aspect of this has been the growth of the ESP movement (Robinson 1980) and needs analyses (Munby 1978). Another has been the concern for the individualization of instruction (Altman and James 1980; Geddes and Sturtridge 1982). However, each of these trends has, rather curiously, sidestepped the actual learner. With ESP, there has been a preoccupation with needs, as opposed to *wants* (Skehan 1984b), and there has been a conflation of means and ends (Widdowson 1983), with insufficient attention to how terminal competence is to be achieved. The individualization movement contrasts sharply with this, in that it has produced large quantities of attractive and stimulating materials. The aim seems to have been the provision of choice, but this has generally been choice for its own sake, rather than principled choice linked to learner characteristics. The findings discussed in this book, however, argue for research connecting individualized materials, whether ESP or general, to characteristics of the learner, so that one can examine the degree of match between the two, and as a result, increase the effectiveness of the materials, rather than relying on chance factors.

13: Cognitive style and personality variables account for very little of the variance in language achievement tests

(Chapter 6): The evidence for cognitive style suggests that there is a weak relationship, on the borderline of significance, between field-independence and language learning success. There is also the problem of deciding how separate cognitive style is from related learner characteristics, e.g. intelligence and components of language aptitude. With personality, once again significant results are hard to come by, and are matched by failures to find significant effects. There are suggestions that both extroversion and introversion have positive and negative features, and that simple relationships will not be found, condition-seeking designs being needed to tease out the effects concerned.

14 We need to use interaction and condition-seeking designs much more extensively:

(Chapter 7): Quite a number of generalizations can now be proposed about the various IDs taken singly. What we are badly in need of is a sustained programme to fill in the gaps with the potential interactions that have not been investigated. The findings that we have already suggest that significant increases in the efficiency of instruction could be achieved by matching learners with appropriate instructional conditions.

Individual differences and theory construction

In Chapter 1 various models of language learning were discussed and finally the taxonomic model from Naiman *et al*. (1978) was chosen as a useful framework within which to locate ID studies. (The model was then slightly modified in Chapter 7.) This section will discuss the Naiman model and the findings from ID research, relating both of these to theory construction in second language learning.

It is useful, first of all, to look again at the main types of theory that exist in second language learning. McLaughlin (1987) and Larsen-Freeman and Long (in press) both discuss, at length, causal-process theories. Such theories aim at explanation in some area by using sets of definitions, linked by logical deduction to sets of statements which, in some way, model some causal process. The central core of the theory may be abstract and unobservable, but it should permit the deduction of testable statements which relate to the real world, even though the underlying causal agents for actual observable events may be only theoretical contructs. Causal process (or hierarchical, or theory-then-research) approaches have many important advantages. They usually represent the 'best attempt' currently available to explain some area, and so hold out the prospect of being maximally satisfactory. Equally important, there are a number of criteria which can be used to evaluate such theories. One such is internal coherence – the extent to which the components of the theory relate to one another logically, and the extent to which the deductions that are made about the real world are valid deductions. Another criterion for causal process theories is that they should make predictions. The underlying core of the theory, itself abstract and consisting of relationships between hypothetical constructs, should make contact with the real world, by making predictions about it. There is also the criterion of falsifiability, i.e. that hypotheses and deductions from a theory should be capable of disproof. Theories are unsatisfactory if they contain constructs so elastic as to accommodate any set of research findings. Finally (and for the moment, only briefly), a final criterion is that a theory should have a beneficial effect upon additional research. In other words, a good theory should have a systematizing influence upon research, and should increase the chances that cumulative progress will be made.

Four shortcomings of causal process theories will be briefly mentioned. First of all, there is a danger that such theories will, in order to be precise and testable, provide oversimplified accounts of the world. They may, with the goal of constructing a model with impeccable causal statements, so restrict the domain of applicability, or the potential for generalization back to the real world, that the theory concerned may be trivial. Second (and to be developed later), there is the related criticism of theory size. No scale exists to allow us to judge how important or relevant or wide-ranging a theory is, so that once again, an impressive causal-process theory may actually be trivial. Third, there is the possibility that a monolithic theory will become too powerful, and pre-empt research in other directions. Such a theory might take on the mantle of authority and lead to its internal standards being applied outside its domain, or to spurious decisions being made as to what constitutes good research (and is worth funding!). Finally, there is the issue of how readily causal-process theorists are prepared to modify and abandon their theories. They may prefer to modify and patch an original formulation so as to be able to handle discrepant results. It has even been argued (Chalmers 1982) that it is unrealistic to expect very clearly stated theories which lead unequivocally to decisive disconfirmations and that it is more realistic to have a number of predictions which relate in various ways to an underlying core theory. As a result, the attractions of causal process theories, in terms of speed of evaluation and helpfulness for replacement, are seen to be more apparent than real.

The alternative approach to theory construction is generally taken to be a research-then-theory perspective, also known as a concatenated approach to theory building (McLaughlin 1987) or a 'set-of-laws' or 'storehouse' approach (Larsen-Freeman and Long in press). This approach conforms largely to an inductive view of the philosophy of science (Chalmers 1982) and searches for regularities in a particular area. These generalizations then become the laws which can be the basis for more refined research at greater levels of detail. Alternatively they can be the input for further theory building. From the ID domain one could propose 'laws' such as:

- aptitude test scores correlate predictably with end-of-course achievement on language courses with a tendency to yield higher correlations with intensive teaching to heterogeneous students (and vice versa).
- attitude and motivation indices obtained in Canadian anglophone secondary schools enter into correlations with achievement around the 0.40 level.
- extroversion is linked, to some degree, to performance on natural communicative language tasks, while introversion is more linked to performance on language-like tasks.

These ID 'laws' are arranged in order of generality and lack of qualifying statement. The first, about aptitude, relies on the largest number of research studies, and draws upon research carried out in wide variety of settings. As an inductive generalization, it therefore has the greatest probability of being confirmed in future research, without there being *much* restriction on the future settings to be investigated. The motivation 'law', in contrast, is qualified already in terms of Canadian anglophone secondary schools. The implication of this is that one moves outside the restrictions at one's peril: non-Canadian, non-anglophone, and non-secondary variations could each lead to results which are, to some degree, different. The 'extroversion' law is even more qualifed, and the 'to some degree' is a reflection of the fact that this generalization is recent, and has not been widely and repeatedly tested.

Concatenated theories, too, have their strengths and weaknesses. The first advantage is that there are fewer preconceptions, and there is a fairly direct route allowing researchers to draw upon their experience to formulate tentative generalizations which can then be subjected to a process of testing and extension. Such generalizations, once established, could then be the basis for more extensive and sophisticated theory development. Concatenated approaches to research also encourage good instrumentation, in that they foster the development of observational, descriptive and testing instruments which are fairly close to the data and may therefore have general applicability.

The weaknesses of a concatenated approach are, unfortunately, all too apparent. Foremost amongst these is the piecemeal, unsystematic way in which knowledge is extended. This is dependent on the 'laws' that investigators accumulate. The problem is that these laws need not, and in practice usually do not, have any relationship to one another. The examples given earlier illustrate this point. Even those from an ID framework only have in common that they concern IDs. As a result, the research-then-theory approach can simply degenerate into purposeless fact accumulation. In themselves, the 'laws' only describe, and cannot illuminate. A further problem with this approach is that, whatever its claims, it cannot actually be theory-neutral. Any investigation is going to contain some presuppositions and implicit theory, and it would be better to recognize this. This particularly applies to any observation that is carried out, since observation involves some selection of data to be focused on, and measuring instrument to be employed.

Long (1985 p.393) provides a telling illustration of the difference between causal-process and set-of-laws theories.

Conducting research to understand SLA is like trying to make a picture by assembling the pieces of a jigsaw puzzle, but when you have reason to suspect that the pieces in view have been mixed with pieces from other puzzles too . . . You are faced, then, with trying to decide what the final picture looks like, and not knowing which the relevant pieces are. How to proceed?

Noticing that most pieces you can see are either light blue or dark green, one way is to work with pieces of just those colors, believing that they should fit together somehow, and to ignore pieces of different colors, as well as how the pieces you are working on might eventually fit into the whole picture. Gradually, small sections begin to take shape, and it looks as if you have assembled parts of a beach scene, with the blue sky and green sea. You are still not sure, however, that the small segments of completed sky and sea really come from the same picture. This is the 'research-then-theory' strategy.

Another way is to start by looking at the pieces in view, and to guess that the final picture will be a rural landscape, with blue sky and green fields. Starting work on (say) the fields, you put to one side any pieces whose shape or color have no obvious relevance to assembling a picture of a field. You assume that they are from another puzzle. This is the 'theory-then-research' strategy. The projection it allows as to what the final picture is supposed to look like determines which pieces you select as relevant to work on (only those which could help build a picture of a rural landscape).

When the person working with the other strategy tells you that he or she has put together some pieces which show a green wave breaking on a shore, you are unimpressed because you think he or she is working (albeit successfully) on part of a different picture. Also, you think you know, from the outset, what the final picture will look like, whereas he or she is admittedly very vague about that. On the other hand, you are sometimes worried that you may be ignoring relevant parts of the puzzle, even though you cannot see how they could fit in, and even though the person working on those parts cannot tell you, either. The biggest frustration, or the magic of the exercise, depending how you look at it, is that neither of you will know who was right until one of you solves the puzzle.

This long quotation clarifies the distinction admirably (and is also suggestive of the idea that temperamental differences on the part of researchers may influence which approach they take!). Currently the consensus seems to be that the principled nature of the theory-then-research approach, coupled with the standards it proposes for theory evaluation, make it preferable whenever possible to the unsystematic research-then-theory perspective. Yet, undeniably, most ID research has been of the concatenated type. Even the attempts to sketch out a theory of aptitude and learner types have only been possible as a result of extensive 'law seeking' empirical research. One is left wondering, therefore, whether ID research of this type can, indeed, be justified, or whether, in contrast, the appeal of a theory-then-research perspective is more compelling.

There are two reasons why, I feel, ID research is very important and should be conducted on a greater scale than it has been recently. The first of these comes from the need to establish the size of the problem. If we return to the jigsaw analogy, I would like to propose adding, to Long's two problems (deciding on the final picture, and knowing which pieces are relevant) a third – determining how big the jigsaw is. After all, knowing how large the jigsaw is (not to mention the scale of the picture) will be an important clue to how much it is likely to contain. The difficulty with the causal-process approach is that we often do not know the scale of applicability of the theory concerned. We can envisage, that is, someone developing a neat theory about a rural scene, only to discover later that it is about a view out of a window in *part* of the jigsaw. The difficulty, essentially, is that the advantage of having criteria for theory evaluation is that they apply to the *inner* workings of theories. We have less information on the scale of theories or the relationship of different theories to one another. (This is partly the reason why we seem to have a number of theories around in second language learning, and insufficient basis for comparison between them.) I am proposing, that is, that ID research, since it operates on a fairly large scale, is useful for establishing the scale of the problem that we face. Simple-minded models such as that shown in Figure 1.3 and Figure 7.1 may not have much explanatory adequacy but they can more easily cover the range of influences on language learning.

The second justification for ID research concerns the need to make cumulative progress (a quality usually associated with causal-process theories (see Larsen-Freeman and Long in press)). At the outset, it is helpful to make a further distinction between criteria for theory assessment which allow judgements to be made now, and those which can only be used retrospectively. In the first category we have criteria such as internal consistency, parsimony, elegance, explanation, and falsifiability. In the latter, we have, basically, the value of the research programme that a theory generates. The difficulty stems from the fact that many have assumed that generative power derives from the clarity of the theory concerned and how fruitful its predictions are for future research. The problem is that we are rarely in a position to make such judgements. Most of the time the productivity of a research programme can only be judged retrospectively when we see which theories have stood the test of time, and have continued to occupy researchers.

I would like to suggest that the sort of model presented in Figure 7.1, and the discussion of it presented in Chapter 7 provide enough of a framework to maximize the chances that systematic, cumulative progress will be made. The model is rudimentary in explanatory terms, but it does provides a coherent framework for the investigation of quantitative relationships between the variables. It would enable new results to be slotted into the model fairly easily. It is also capable of generating, not specific explanatory predictions, but guidelines as to where research could most usefully be done, or is most urgently needed (see below). As such the framework is more likely to systematize progress and enable investigators to move backwards and forwards from the large perspective of the entire model to the more fine-grained studies they are personally concerned with. Given the current state of knowledge in second language research, such an approach is necessary to provide a springboard for subsequent causal-process theorizing.

Additional research

The final part of the book will look towards the future and areas where ID research may be profitably conducted. There will be two main sections to this discussion. The first will consider some general research principles, while the second will examine specific research areas.

Four main conclusions are warranted on the general nature of ID research. These are the need for better research designs; the need for replication; the need for more longitudinal studies, and the need for more interaction studies. As regards the first of these, we have seen that ID research is close to an inductive view of science, which searches for generalizations and range of applicability. Ideally, one would like a 'theory of situations' to help one predict how different ID traits vary in their influence. Of course, there is no such theory. But from the range of ID research which has been completed, we are now beginning to see some systematicity in variation, and develop some idea of the sorts of variables which need to be controlled. These include:

- the nature of the criterion measure: especially communicative vs. language-like performance
- the age of the learners: especially young children (<10) vs. adolescents and adults
- the setting: foreign language vs. naturalistic
- data sources on ID variables: especially test and questionnaire based vs. observational and self-report
- language status relationships: majority vs. minority, official vs. non-official, unicultural vs. multicultural

Quite possibly not all these factors are important for all ID variables. However, they do need to be taken into account. The basic issue is that of external validity – how generalizable are the results of a particular study? For example, if a study is run which establishes the importance of aptitude with schoolchildren, using multiple-choice achievement tests in a foreign language learning situation (say British children learning French), how confident could we be that a similar result could be obtained if these same children were learning (say) Hindi; or provided with immersion education; or given more communicative tests. We need theory to stitch together the rather isolated and circumscribed 'laws' that have been established. But we also need investigators to be sensitive to these research design issues, and design studies which build in some consideration of these variables with a view to establishing generality of results.

In addition, there is a clear need for the replication of research. Although the quantity of applied linguistic research has grown enormously, there is still a tendency for much of it to be concerned with 'one-shot' studies which do not relate to other theory or research. One problem that then arises is that 'findings' from one study may be widely quoted, even though the original study may have been rather fallible. Given the number of unknown and uncontrolled variables that we have, it could be argued that the greatest priority of all is to ensure that a higher proportion of studies are subjected to replication.

Next (and rather traditionally, in exhortation sections such as this), there needs to be a plea for more longitudinal research. Investigators, quite understandably, tend to aim for efficiency in research designs. However, especially where more affective or strategic IDs are concerned, it would be useful to have more naturalistic, more observational, more self-report and *longer-term* data which would provide us with an insider's perspective on the learning, and give a more dynamic picture which might be revealing about the patterns of causation involved over time.

Finally, and developing the point about better research designs, we need to have more studies which build in condition-seeking facets to the design. It is now naive if one looks simply for main effects without considering the ways in which combinations of variables might operate. Classroom-based insights into learning success invariably focus on how combinations of circumstances produce results, rather than individual variables taken singly. As a result, investigators will need to build in such conditions routinely. They will also need to familiarize themselves with techniques such as two- and three-way analysis of variance designs, and generalized regression analysis (McLaughlin 1980). Only such approaches will do justice to the complexity of language learning.

We turn next to a consideration of specific research that could be conducted. Two main types of research seem indicated with language aptitude. First, we need to use a wider conception of communicative competence as a target for aptitude test prediction, in order to stimulate research that investigates relevant aptitudes for sociolinguistic, discourse, and pragmatic components of communicative competence. Current conceptions of aptitude have been exclusively linguistic. Even though such aptitudes are probably relevant for informal situations communicative competence is clearly more wide-ranging, and so, therefore, should be aptitude research.

The second major area for aptitude research is to make better connections with psycholinguistic and acquisitional traditions in applied linguistics. The three-component view of aptitude (phonemic coding ability; language analytic capacity; and memory) could be taken to represent the stages in the perception, analysis, and then storage and retrieval of information as it passes through the human information processing system. There is scope for additional research here which might be revealing about whether language learning ability does, to some degree, relate to autonomous language capacities or whether they are simply an extension of general cognitive abilities. Similarly, one could relate aptitude to acquisitional processes. Current SLA research focuses upon processes and universals. But quite clearly, there are wide IDs in language learning performance. Given the generalizations emerging from the SLA literature, e.g. invariance of developmental sequences, and resistance of developmental sequences to alteration by instruction, it would be interesting to see whether the aptitude variable, especially the language analytic component, is implicated. Do high-aptitude students make different types of error? Are they more responsive to correction? Does instruction have an effect with them if not with others? Are they less systematic in developmental sequences?

The area of motivation, too, contains considerable potential for research. Above all, it would be helpful if a framework could be developed into which the various motivation studies could fit. This would mean going outside the 'internal motivation of the learner' approach and incorporating other influences, such as external pressures, examinations, intrinsic interest of learning, etc., which could interact with an autonomous motivation. It should also allow a clearer understanding of the effects of the different situations and contexts in which language learning takes place on motivational orientation. The other issue facing motivation research is that of establishing the direction of causation. We have seen that Strong (1984) proposes reversing the direction of causation advocated by Gardner (1985). In this respect motivation is a clear case illustrating some of the research precepts discussed earlier. A longitudinal approach is needed, combining observational and introspective data, which allows the investigator some access to the fluctuating states of learner motivation that must surely operate. At present, we are working with an approach similar to a series of still photographs, the connections between which have to be inferred. To resolve the issue of causality, we need something which is more continuous and dynamic, as well as more open in the categories that it uses.

In Chapter 5, we saw how much work has been done in the learning strategies area, but also how little systematicity there is. The consequence of this is that there is wide scope for additional research. We need to be more systematic in collecting data on young children, secondary school children, and adults, to determine how comparable these groups are. Similarly, the setting for learning, i.e. foreign language vs.

naturalistic, could also benefit from more ordered comparison. There could also be greater systematicity in data collection. Currently, different investigators have used a variety of techniques. It would be very helpful to know how these different sorts of measure relate to one another, and whether any of them introduce systematic biases so as to influence the data that are being collected. The other major area which requires research is that of strategy training. We need a wider range of strategies as the basis for training. It is quite likely that not all strategies are equally susceptible to training, and so we need to run careful studies to discover which are most modifiable. A parallel need would be to investigate the conditions of instruction for strategy training. It may be more difficult than has been previously thought to convey to learners what different strategies involve, and how they can become habits. The development of effective instructional techniques here, as well as exploring how much time is needed to produce strategy change, should be priorities.

The area of personality and cognitive style (Chapter 6) seems to be at a more preliminary and fragmented stage than some of the other areas of ID research, and this is reflected in the sort of research that is most needed. First of all, there is a need for research in which contaminating variables, especially those relating to criterion measures, are controlled more carefully. The generalizations that exist are tentative at present, and need to be established more clearly, e.g. the role of extroversion in learning. Second, there is scope, in many areas, for the development of better or at least more varied measurement techniques. It would seem that the area of miscellaneous personality traits is one that is particularly susceptible to measurement effects, and it may be that self-report and questionnaire methods of data elicitation do not tally with actual behaviour. Finally, there is a great need to define constructs so that they can be distinguished from one another, and then validate the measurement techniques that are derived from such definitions, e.g. outgoingness, sociability, social competence, and risk taking need to be distinguished in this way from one another and from extroversion.

Finally, we come to the study of interaction effects. In some ways there is little specific to add in this section. What is needed, above all, is a considerable quantity of additional research which fills out the framework discussed in Chapter 7. In addition, perhaps, it is worth mentioning that since we are now looking for interactions between learner IDs and classroom and situational variables, it is important for ID researchers to become well versed in the advances that are being made descriptively and theoretically in these other areas. Classroom observation instruments need to be used extensively in condition-seeking research, as do insights into syllabus construction, methodology analysis, and the evaluation of teaching. And finally, perhaps, condition-seeking research has not distinguished itself by the breadth of the language achievement and proficiency measures that it has used. Given the trend towards a communicative approach to language teaching, this is a mistake that must be soon remedied.

Conclusions

Individual difference research, as this volume has shown, has substantial accomplishments to its credit, and contains several independent and thriving research traditions. Yet it has been an area of neglect, and has not been sufficiently integrated into mainstream SLA studies. This final chapter has argued that there are several areas where ID research is urgently needed. More fundamentally, it has argued that such research is necessary from a theory-building perspective since it is more likely to enable the broad outlines of second and foreign language learning research to be established, and consequently to provide an evaluative framework for more small-scale and theory-driven work to be located. As such ID research is an important frontier area – capable of synthesizing and integrating the more fine-grained research done elsewhere.

References

Abraham R.G. (1985) 'Field independence-dependence and the teaching of grammar', *TESOL Quarterly*, 20, 4, 689–702.

Al-Haik A.R. (1972), *Exploring the auditory aspects of aptitude for intensive modern foreign language learning*, Unpublished Ph.D. dissertation, University of California at Berkeley.

Allen J.P.B. and Davies A. (eds.) (1977), *Testing and Experimental Methods: The Edinburgh Course in Applied Linguistics, Vol. 4*, Oxford: Oxford University Press.

Allen J.P.B., Frohlich M., and Spada N. (1984), 'The communicative orientation of language teaching', In Handscombe J., Orem R., and Taylor B. (eds.) *On TESOL '83: The Question of Control* Washington, DC: TESOL.

Altman H.B. and James C.V. (eds.) (1980) *Foreign Language Teaching: Meeting Individual Needs*, Oxford: Pergamon Press.

Anderson J.R. (1985) *Cognitive Psychology and its Implications*, New York: W.H. Freeman & Co.

Bachman L. and Palmer A. (1981), 'The construct validation of some components of communicative proficiency', *TESOL Quarterly*, 16, 4, 449–65.

Baddeley A. and Hitch G. (1974), 'Working memory', in Bower G. (1974), *The Psychology of Learning and Motivation*, Vol. 8, New York: Academic Press.

Bailey K.M. (1983) 'Competitiveness and anxiety in adult second language learning: Looking *at* and *through* the diary studies', In Seliger and Long (1983).

Bartley D.E. (1969), 'A pilot study of aptitude and attitude factors in language dropout', *California Journal of Educational Research*, 20, 48–55.

—— (1970), 'The importance of the attitude factor in language dropout: A preliminary investigation of group and sex differences', *Foreign Language Annals*, 3, 383–93.

Beebe L. (1983), 'Risk-taking and the language learner', in Seliger and Long (1983).

Bem D.J. (1971), 'The concept of risk in the study of human behaviour', In Carney R.E. (ed.), *Risk-taking Behaviour*, Springfield, Ill: Charles C. Thomas.

Bialystok E. (1978), 'A theoretical model of second language learning', *Language Learning*, 28, 69–83.

—— (1979), 'The role of conscious strategies in second language proficiency', *Canadian Modern Language Review*, 35, 372–394.

—— (1981), 'Some evidence for the integrity and interaction of two knowledge sources', In R. Andersen (ed.), *New Dimensions in Second Language*

Acquisition Research, Rowley, Mass.: Newbury House.
—— (in preparation), *Communication Strategies*.
—— and Frohlich M. (1977), 'Aspects of second language learning in classroom settings', *Working Papers in Bilingualism*, 13, 1–26.
—— (1978), 'The aural grammar test: Description and implications', *Working Papers on Bilingualism*, 15, 15–35.
Bolinger D. (1975) 'Meaning and memory', *Forum Linguisticum*, 1, 2–14.
Brown A.L. and Palinscar A.S. (1982), 'Inducing strategic learning from texts by means of informed self-control training', *Topics in Learning and Learning Disabilities*, 2, 1–17.
Brown H.D. (1987), *Principles of Language Learning and Teaching* (2nd edn), Englewood Cliffs, NJ: Prentice-Hall.
Brown R.W. (1986), *Social Psychology: The Second Edition*, New York: The Free Press.
Burstall C. (1975) 'Factors affecting foreign language learning: A consideration of some recent research findings', *Language Teaching Abstracts*, 1–21.
—— Jamieson M., Cohen S. and Hargreaves M. (1974), *Primary French in the Balance*, Slough: NFER.
Canale M. (1983), 'On some dimensions of language proficiency', In Oller (1983).
—— and Swain M. (1980) 'Theoretical bases of communicative approaches to second language teaching and testing', *Applied Linguistics*, 1, 1, 1–47.
Carroll J.B. (1965), 'The prediction of success in foreign language training', In R. Glaser (ed.), *Training, Research, and Education*, New York: Wiley.
—— (1973), 'Implications of aptitude test research and psycholinguistic theory for foreign language teaching', *International Journal of Psycholinguistics*, 2, 5–14.
—— (1979), 'Psychometric approaches to the study of language abilities', In Fillmore C.J. *et al.* (1979).
—— (1981), 'Twenty-five years of research on foreign language aptitude', In Diller K.C. (ed.) (1981).
—— (1983), 'Psychometric theory and language testing', In Oller (1983).
—— and Sapon S. (1959) *Modern Languages Aptitude Test – Form A*, New York: The Psychological Corporation.
—— (1967) *Modern Languages Aptitude Test – Elementary*, New York: The Psychological Corporation.
—— and Spearritt D. (1967), 'A study of "A Model of School Learning" ' Unpublished report, Graduate School of Education, Harvard University, (ED 045477), Cited in Cronbach L. and Snow R. (1977), *Aptitudes and Instructional Methods*, New York: Irvington.
Cathcart R. (1986), 'Input generation by young second language learners', *TESOL Quarterly*, 20, 3, 515–30.
Chalmers A.F. (1982), *What is this Thing called Science?*, Milton Keynes: Open University Press.
Chamot A.U. and O'Malley J.M. (1987), 'The cognitive academic language learning approach: A bridge to the mainstream', *TESOL Quarterly*, 21, 2, 227–49.
Chapelle C. and Jamieson J. (1986), 'Computer assisted language learning as a

predictor of success in acquiring English as a Second Language', *TESOL Quarterly*, 20, 1, 27–46.

Chastain K. (1975), 'Affective and ability factors in second language acquisition', *Language Learning*, 25, 1, 153–61.

Chesterfield R. and Chesterfield K.B. (1985), 'Natural order in children's use of second language learning strategies', *Applied Linguistics*, 6, 1.

Chihara T. and Oller J. (1978), 'Attitudes and attained proficiency in EFL: A sociolinguistic study of adult Japanese speakers', *Language Learning*, 28, 55–68.

Clark H. and Clark E. (1977), *Psychology and Language: An Introduction to Psycholinguistics*, New York: Harcourt Brace Jovanovitch.

Clement R. (1980), 'Ethnicity, contact, and communicative competence in a second language', In Giles H., Robinson W.P., and Smith P.M. (eds.), *Language: Social Psychological Perspectives*, Oxford: Pergamon.

—— (1986), 'Second language proficiency and acculturation: An investigation of the effects of language status and individual characteristics', *Journal of Language and Social Psychology*, 5, 4, 271–90.

—— and Kruidenier B. (1983) 'Orientations in second language acquisition: 1. The effects of ethnicity, milieu, and target language on their emergence', *Language Learning*, 33, 3, 273–91.

—— and Kruidenier B. (1985) 'Aptitude, attitude, and motivation in second language proficiency: A test of Clement's model', *Journal of Language and Social Psychology*, 4, 1, 21–37.

——, Gardner R.C. and Smythe P.C. (1977), 'Motivational variables in second language acquisition: A study of Francophones learning English', *Canadian Journal of Behavioural Sciences*, 9, 2, 123–33.

——, Gardner R.C., and Smythe P.D. (1980), 'Social and individual factors in second language acquisition', *Canadian Journal of Behavioural Sciences*, 12, 4, 293–302.

—— Smythe P.C. and Gardner R.C. (1978), 'Persistence in second language study: motivational considerations', *Canadian Modern Language Review*, 34, 688–94.

Clifford R. (1981), 'Convergent and discriminant validation of integrated and unitary language skills: the need for a research model', in Palmer A., Groot P.J.M., and Trosper G.A., *The Construct Validation of Tests of Communicative Competence*, Washington, DC: TESOL.

Coan R.W. and Cattell R.B. (1966), *Early School Personality Questionnaire*, Champaign, Illinois: Institute for Personality and Ability Testing.

Cohen A.D. (1983), 'Studying second-language learning strategies: How do we get the information?', *Applied Linguistics*, 5, pp. 101–12.

Corder S.P. (1973), *Introducing Applied Linguistics*, Harmondsworth: Penguin.

Craik F.I.M. and Lockhart R.S. (1972), 'Levels of processing: A framework for memory research', *Journal of Verbal Learning and Verbal Behaviour*, 11, 671–84.

Culhane P.T. (ed.) (1971), *Occasional Paper No. 7*, Colchester, England: University of Essex Language Centre.

Davies A. (1971a), 'Aptitude for and proficiency in French in the first year of the UK secondary school', In Perren G.E. and Trim J.L.M. (eds.) *Applica-*

tions of Linguistics, Cambridge University Press.

—— (1971b), 'Language aptitude in the first year of the UK secondary school', *RELC Journal*, 2, 1.

—— (1978), Language testing', *Language Teaching and Linguistics Abstracts*, 11, 145–59 and 215–31. Reprinted in V. Kinsella (ed.) (1982) *Surveys*, Cambridge University Press.

Day R.R. (ed.) (1986), *Talking to Learn: Conversation in Second Language Acquisition*, Rowley, Mass.: Newbury House.

Dickensen L. (1987) *Self-instruction in Language Learning*, Cambridge University Press.

Dickson P., Boyce C., Lee B., Portal M., and Smith M. (1985), *Foreign Language Performance in Schools: Report on the 1983 survey of French, German, and Spanish*, London: Department of Education and Science.

Diller K.C. (ed.) (1981), *Individual Differences and Universals in Language Learning Aptitude*, Rowley, Mass.: Newbury House.

Donaldson M. (1978), *Children's Minds*, London: Penguin.

Dulay H.C., Burt M.K. and Krashen S.D. (1982), *Language Two*, New York: Oxford University Press.

Eckman F.R., Bell L.H., and Nelson D. (1984), *Universals of Second Language Acquisition*, Rowley, Mass.: Newbury House.

Ellis G. and Sinclair B. (1987), *Training for Learners of English* (Pilot Edition), Cambridge University Press.

Ely C.M. (1986), 'An analysis of discomfort, risktaking, sociability, and motivation in the L2 classroom', *Language Learning*, 36, 1, 1–25.

Entwistle N.J. and Entwistle D.M. (1970), 'The relationship between personality, study methods, and academic performance', *British Journal of Educational Psychology*, 40, 132–41.

—— and Wilson J.D. (1977), *Degrees of Excellence: The Academic Achievement Game*, London: Hodder & Stoughton.

Everitt B. (1978), *Cluster Analysis*, (2nd edn), London: Heinemann Educational.

Eysenck H.J. (1957), *Dynamics of anxiety and hysteria*, London: Routledge & Kegan Paul.

—— (1965), *Fact and Fiction in Psychology*, Harmondsworth: Penguin.

—— (1970), *The Structure of Human Personality*, London: Routledge & Kegan Paul.

Faerch C. and Kasper G. (1983), *Strategies for Interlanguage Communication*, London: Longman.

Farhady H. (1983), 'On the plausibility of the unitary language proficiency factor', In Oller (1983).

Ferencich M. (ed.) (1964), *Reattivo di attitudine linguistica*, Florence: Organizzazioni Speciali.

Fillmore C.J., Kempler D., and Wang W-S.Y. (eds.) (1979), *Individual Differences in Language Ability and Language Behaviour*, New York: Academic Press.

Gallegos A.M. (1968), 'A study and comparison of experimenter pacing and student pacing of programmed instruction', *Journal of Education Research*, 61, 339–42.

Gardner R.C. (1979), 'Social-psychological aspects of second language acquisition', In Giles H. and St. Clair R. (eds.) *Language and Social Psychology*, Oxford: Blackwell.

—— (1980), 'On the validity of affective variables in second language acquisition: conceptual, contextual, and statistical considerations', *Language Learning*, 30, 255–70.

—— (1985), *Social Psychology and Second Language Learning: The Role of Attitudes and Motivation*, London: Edward Arnold.

—— Clement R., Smythe P.C. and Smythe C.L. (1979), *Attitude and Motivation Test Battery – Revised Manual*, Research Bulletin No. 15, Language Research Group, Department of Psychology, University of Western Ontario.

—— and Gliksman L. (1982), 'On "Gardner on affect": A discussion of validity as it relates to the Attitude/Motivation Test Battery: A response from Gardner', *Language Learning*, 32, 1, 191–200.

——, Lalonde R.N., and Moorcroft R. (1985), 'The role of attitudes and motivation in second language learning: Correlational and experimental considerations', *Language Learning*, 35, 2, 207–27.

—— and Lambert W.E. (1959), 'Motivational variables in second language acquisition', *Canadian Journal of Psychology*, 13, 266–72.

—— and Lambert W.E. (1972), *Attitudes and Motivation in Second Language Learning*, Rowley, Mass.: Newbury House.

——, Smythe P.D. and Clement R. (1979), 'Intensive second language study in a bicultural milieu: an investigation of attitudes, motivation, and language proficiency', *Language Learning*, 29, 2, 305–20.

—— and Smythe P.D. (1981), 'On the development of the Attitude/Motivation Test Battery', *Canadian Modern Language Review*, 37, 510–25.

——, Smythe P.D., Clement R., and Gliksman L. (1976), 'Second language learning: A social-psychological perspective', *Canadian Modern Language Review*, 32,. 198–213.

Gass S. and Madden C. (1985), *Input in Second Language Acquisition*, Rowley, Mass.: Newbury House.

Geddes M. and Sturtridge G. (1982), *Individualisation*, London: Modern English Publications.

Genessee F. and Hamayan E. (1980), 'Individual differences in second language learning', *Applied Psycholinguistics*, 1, 95–110.

Gliksman L. (1976), *Second language acquisition: the effects of student attitudes on classroom behaviour*, Unpublished MA thesis, University of Western Ontario.

Goldin-Meadow S., (1982), 'The resilience of recursion: A study of a communication system developed without a conventional language model', In Wanner E. and Gleitman L. (eds.), *Language Acquisition: The state of the art*, Cambridge University Press.

Gorsuch R.L. (1974), *Factor Analysis*, Philadelphia: Saunders.

Gregg K. (1984), 'Krashen's Monitor and Occam's Razor', *Applied Linguistics*, 5, 79–100.

Green P.S. (1975a), *The Language Laboratory in School: The York Study*, Edinburgh: Oliver & Boyd.

—— (1975b), 'Aptitude testing: an ongoing experiment', *Audio-Visual Language Journal*, 12, 205–10.

Greene J.C. (1985), 'Relationships among learning and attribution theory variables', *American Educational Research Journal*, 22, 1, 65–78.

Hansen J. and Stansfield C. (1981), 'The relationship of field dependent–independent cognitive styles to foreign language achievement', *Language Learning*, 31, 2, 349–67.

Hansen L. (1984), 'Field dependence–independence and language testing. Evidence from six Pacific Island cultures', *TESOL Quarterly*, 18, 2, 311–24.

Hassall S. (1984), 'An application of "The Good Language Learner" to EFL learners in Bahrain', *TESOL France Newsletter* vol. 5, pp. 15–23.

Hatch E.M. and Farhady H. (1983), *Research Design and Statistics for Applied Linguistics*, Rowley, Mass.: Newbury House.

Henmon V.A.C., Bohan J.E., and Brigham C.C. (1929), *Prognosis tests in modern foreign languages*, New York: Macmillan.

Henning G. (1987), *A Guide to Language Testing: Development, Evaluation, Research*, Rowley, Mass.: Newbury House.

Hermann G. (1980), 'Attitudes and success in children's learning of English as a Second Language: The motivational vs. resultative hypothesis', *English Language Teaching Journal*, 34, 247–54.

Hosenfeld C. (1977), 'A preliminary investigation of the reading strategies of successful and non-successful language learners', *System*, 5, 110–23.

Huang X-H and Van Naerssen M. (1985), 'Learning strategies for oral communication', *Applied Linguistics*, 6, 287–307.

Hubbard L.J. (1975), 'Aptitude, attitude, and sensitivity', *Foreign Language Annals*, 8, 33–7.

Huebner T. (1985), 'System and variability in interlanguage syntax', *Language Learning*, 35, 2, 141–63.

Hymes D. (1970), 'On communicative competence', in Gumperz J. and Hymes D. (eds.) *Directions in Sociolinguistics*, New York: Holt, Rinehart, & Winston.

Jones C.L., Mackintosh H. and McPherson A.P. (1973), 'Questions of uncertainty: non-cognitive predictors of achievement', In Page C.F. and Gibson J. (eds.), *Motivation: Non-Cognitive Aspects of Student Performance*, London: SRHE.

Joreskog K.G. and Sorbum D. (1981), *LISREL V: User's Guide*, Chicago: National Educational Resources.

Kaplan J. and Shand M. (1984), 'Error detection as a function of integrativity', In Eckman (ed.) (1984).

Kim J-O and Mueller T. (1978), *Introduction to Factor Analysis: What it is and how to do it*, Beverley Hills, Cal. Sage Publications.

Krashen S.D. (1981a), 'Aptitude and attitude in relation to second language acquisition and learning', In Diller (ed.) (1981).

—— (1981b), *Second Language Acquisition and Second Language Learning*, Oxford: Pergamon.

—— (1985), *The Input Hypothesis*, London: Longman.

Kruidenier B.G. and Clement R. (1986), *The Effect of Context on the Composition and Role of Orientations in Second Language Acquisition*, International Centre for Research on Bilingualism, Quebec.

Levinson S. (1983), *Pragmatics*, Cambridge University Press.

Larsen-Freeman D. and Long M.H. (forthcoming), *An Introduction to Second*

Language Acquisition Research, London: Longman.

Linday P. and Norman D. (1977), *Human Information Processing*, New York: Academic Press.

Long J.S. (1983a), *Convariance Structure Models: An introduction to LISREL*, London: Sage Publications.

—— (1983b), *Confirmatory Factor Analysis*, London: Sage Publications.

Long M.H. (1983a), 'Inside the "Black Box": Methodological issues in classroom research on language learning', In Seliger and Long (eds) (1983).

—— (1983b), 'Native speaker non-native speaker conversation and the negotiation of comprehensible input', *Applied Linguistics*, 4, 2, 126–41.

—— (1985), 'Input and second language acquisition theory' In Gass S. and Madden C. (1985).

—— (in press), 'Instructed interlanguage development', In Beebe L. (ed.) *Issues in Second Language Acquisition: Multiple Perspectives*, Rowley, Mass.: Newbury House.

Lukmani Y. (1972), 'Motivation to learn and learning proficiency', *Language Learning*, 22, 261–73.

McClelland D.C. (1958), 'Risk taking in children with high and low need for achievement', In Atkinson J.W. (ed.), *Motives in Fantasy, Action, and Society*, Princeton, NJ: Van Nostrand.

—— (1961), *The Achieving Society*, Princeton, NJ: Van Nostrand.

—— Atkinson J.W., Clark R.A. and Lowell E.L. (1953), *The Achievement Motive*, New York: Appleton, Century, Crofts.

McDonough S.H. (1981), *Psychology in Foreign Language Teaching*, London: George Allen & Unwin.

McLaughlin B. (1978), 'The monitor model: Some methodological considerations', *Language Learning*, 28, 309–32.

—— (1980), 'Theory and research in second language learning: An emerging paradigm', *Language Learning*, 30, 331–50.

—— (1987), *Theories of Second Language Learning*, London: Edward Arnold.

Maier M.H. and Jacobs P.I. (1966), 'The effect of variations in self-instructional progam on instructional outcomes', *Psychological Reports*, 18, 539–46.

Mandler G. (1967), 'Verbal learning', In Mandler G., Mussen P., Kogan N. and Wallach M. *New Directions in Psychology*, New York: Holt, Rinehart & Winston.

—— (1979), 'Organisation and repetition', In Nilsson L.G. (ed.), *Perspectives in Memory Research*, Hillsdale, NJ: Lawrence Erlbaum.

Mehrabian A. (1968), 'Male and female scales of the tendency to achieve', *Educational and Psychological Measurement*, 28, 493–502.

Meisel J. (1980), 'Linguisitic simplification', In Felix S. (ed.) *Second Language Development: Trends and Issues*, Tubingen: Narr.

Milanovic M. (1988), *The Construction and Validation of a Performance-based Battery of English Language progress Tests*, Unpublished Ph.D. dissertation, University of London.

Mitchell R., Parkinson B., and Johnstone R. (1981), *The Foreign Language Classroom: An Observational Study*, Stirling Monographs No. 9: Stirling University.

Mowrer O.H. (1950), *Learning Theory and Personality Dynamics*, New York: Ronald.

Munby J. (1978), *Communicative Syllabus Design*, Cambridge University Press.

Murakami K. (1974), 'A language aptitude test for the Japanese', *System*, 2, 3, 31–47.

Naiman N., Frohlich M., Stern H.H., Todesco A. (1978), *The Good Language Learner*, Research in Education Series, 7. Ontario Institute for Studies in Education.

Natelson E.R. (1975), *The predictive validity of each of the five parts of the MLAT: The effect of previous language training on MLAT scores: The correlation of MLAT scores and achievement in specific language groups*, Unpublished Ph.d. dissertation: Dissertation Abstracts.

Nation R. and McLaughlin B. (1986), 'Experts and novices: an information processing approach to the "good language learner" problem', *Applied Psycholinguistics*, 7, 41–56.

Nelson K. (1981), 'Individual differences in language development: implications for development and language', *Developmental Psychology*, 17, 170–87.

Neufeld G.G. (1978), 'A theoretical perspective on the nature of linguistic aptitude', *International Review of Applied Linguistics*, 16, 15–25.

Norusis M.J. (1986), *SPSS/PC +*: Advanced Statistics, Chicago, Illinois: SPSS Inc.

O'Malley J.M., Chamot A.U., Stewner-Manzares G., Kupper L. and Russo R.P. (1985a), 'Learning strategies used by beginning and intermediate ESL students', *Language Learning*, 35, 1, 21–46.

——, Chamot A.U., Stewner-Manzares G., Kupper L. and Russo R.P. (1985b), 'Learning strategy applications with students of English as a Second Language', *TESOL Quarterly*, 19, 285–96.

Oller J.W. (1977), 'Attitude variables in second language learning', In Burt M., Dulay H. and Finocchiaro M. (eds.) *Viewpoints on English as a Second Language*, New York: Regents.

—— (1981), 'Research on the measurement of affective variables: some remaining questions', In R.W. Andersen (ed.), *New Dimensions in Second Language Acquisition Research*, Rowley, Mass.: Newbury House.

—— (ed.) (1983), *Issues in Language Testing Research*, Rowley, Mass.: Newbury House.

——, Baca L., and Vigil F. (1977), 'Attitudes and attained proficiency in ESL: A sociolinguistic study of Mexican Americans in the Southwest', *TESOL Quarterly*, 11, 173–82.

—— and Perkins K. (1978a), 'Intelligence and language proficiency as sources of variance in self-reported affective variables', *Language Learning*, 28, 1, 85–97.

—— and Perkins K. (1978b), 'A further comment on language proficiency as a source of variance in certain affective measures', *Language Learning*, 28, 2, 417–23.

—— Hudson A.J. and Liu P.F. (1977), 'Attitudes and attained proficiency in ESL: A sociolinguistic study of native speakers of Chinese in the United States', *Language Learning*, 27, 1, 1–25.

Pawley A. and Syder F. (1983), 'Two puzzles for linguistic theory: nativelike selection and nativelike fluency', In Richards J.C. and Schmidt R. (eds.)

Language and Communication, London: Longman.

Pedhazur E.J. (1982), *Multiple Regression in Behavioural Research*, (2nd edn), New York: Holt, Rinehart & Winston.

Peters A. (1983), *Units of Language Acquisition*, Cambridge University Press.

Petersen C.R. and Al-Haik A. (1976), 'The development of the Defense Language Aptitude Battery (DLAB)', *Educational and Psychological Measurement*, 36, 369–80.

Pica T., Doughty C., and Young R. (1986), 'Making input comprehensible: Do interactional modifications help?', *ITL Review of Applied Linguistics*, 72, 1–25.

Pimsleur P. (1966), *The Pimsleur Language Aptitude Battery*, New York: Harcourt, Brace, Jovanovitch.

—— (1968), 'Language aptitude testing', In A. Davies (ed.), *Language Testing Symposium: A Psycholinguistic Perspective*, Oxford: Oxford University Press.

——, Sundland D.M., and McIntyre R.D. (1966), *Underachievement in Foreign Language Learning*, Washington, DC: Modern Language Association.

Politzer R.L. and McGroarty M. (1985), 'An exploratory study of learning behaviours and their relationship to gains in linguistic and communicative competence', *TESOL Quarterly*, 19, 1, 103–23.

—— and Weiss L. (1969), 'An experiment in improving achievement in foreign language learning through learning of selected skills associated with language aptitude', Stanford, Cal: Stanford University. (ERIC Document Reproduction Service, ED 046261).

Pritchard D. (1952), 'An investigation of the relationship of personality traits and ability in modern languages', *British Journal of Educational Psychology*, 22, 147–8.

Reid J.M. (1986), 'Learning style preferences of ESL students', *TESOL Quarterly*, 87–111.

Reves T. (1983), *What makes a good language learners?*, Unpublished Ph.D. thesis, Hebrew University of Jerusalem.

Richards J.C. and Rodgers T.S. (ms), 'Through the looking glass: trends and directions in language teaching', University of Hawaii.

Robinson P. (1980), *English for Specific Purposes*, Oxford: Pergamon.

Rossier R. (1976), *Extroversion-interversion as a significant variable in the learning of oral English as a second language*, Unpublished Ph.D. dissertation, University of Southern California.

Rubin J. (1975), 'What the "Good Language Learner" can teach us', *TESOL Quarterly*, 9, 1, 41–51.

—— (1981), 'Study of cognitive processes in second language learning', *Applied Linguistics*, 117–31.

Sarason S.B. (1958), 'A test anxiety scale for children', *Child Development*, 29, 105–15.

Sato C.J. (1982), 'Ethnic styles in classroom discourse', In Hines M. and Rutherford W. (eds.), *On TESOL '81*, Washington DC: TESOL.

—— (1985), 'Task variation in interlanguage phonology', In Gass and Madden (1985).

Savignon S. (1972), *Communicative Competence: Theory and Classroom Practice*, Reading, Mass.: Addison Wesley.

Schumann J. (1978), 'The acculturation model for second language acquisition', In R.C. Gingras (ed.), *Second Language Acquisition and Foreign Language Teaching*, Arlington, Va.: Center for Applied Linguistics.

Scovel T. (1978), 'The effect of affect on foreign language learning: A review of the anxiety research', *Language Learning*, 28, 129–42.

Seliger H.W. (1983), 'The language learner as linguist: of metaphors and realities', *Applied Linguistics*, 4, 179–91.

—— and Long M.H. (eds.) (1983), *Classroom Oriented Research in Second Language Acquisition*, Rowley, Mass.: Newbury House.

Selinker L. (1972), 'Interlanguage', *International Review of Applied Linguistics*, 10, 209–31.

Skehan P. (1980), 'Memory, language aptitude, and second language performance', *Polyglot*, 2 Fiche 3.

—— (1982) *Memory and motivation in language aptitude testing*, Unpublished Ph.D. thesis, University of London.

—— (1984a), 'On the non-magical nature of foreign language learning', *Polyglot*, 5, Fiche 1.

—— (1984b), 'Issues in the testing of English for Specific Purposes', *Language Testing*, 1, 2, 202–20.

—— (1986a) 'The role of foreign language aptitude in a model of school learning', *Language Testing*, 3, 2, 188–221.

—— (1986b), 'Cluster analysis and the identification of learner types', In V. Cook (ed.) *Experimental approaches to second language acquisition*, Oxford: Pergamon.

—— (1986c) 'Where does language aptitude come from?' In Meara P. (ed.) *Spoken Language*, London: Centre for Information on Language Teaching.

—— (1987), 'Forces for change in language development', Paper presented at the 1987 British Association of Applied Linguistics Conference, Nottingham.

—— (1988), *A Comparison of First and Foreign Language Learning Ability*, ESOL Department, Institute of Education, London University: Working Documents No. 8.

—— (in press, a), 'The relationship between native and foreign language learning ability: Educational and linguistic factors', In Dechert H.W. (ed.), *Current Trends in European Second Language Acquisition Research*, Clevedon, Avon: Multilingual Matters.

—— (in press, b), 'Early lexical development and the prediction of foreign language learning success', In H. Lunt (ed.) *Proceedings of the CILT/ESRC Conference on Second Language Acquisition Research*, London: Centre for Information on Language Teaching.

—— (in press, c) 'Language testing: State of the art review', *Language Teaching Abstracts*, Cambridge University Press.

Smart J.C., Elton C.F., Burnett C.W. (1970), 'Underachievers and over-achievers in intermediate French', *Modern Language Journal*, 54, 415–20.

Spielberger C.D. (ed.) (1966), *Anxiety and Behaviour*, New York: Academic Press.

Spolsky B. (in press), *Conditions for Second Language Learning*, Oxford University Press.

Stern H.H. (1975), 'What can we learn from the good language learner?', *Canadian Modern Language Review*, 31, 304–18.

Strong M.H. (1983), 'Social styles and second language acquisition of Spanish-speaking kindergartners', *TESOL Quarterly*, 17, 2, 241–58.

—— (1984), 'Integrative motivation: Cause or result of successful second language acquisition?', *Language Learning*, 34, 3, 1–14.

Suter R.W. (1976), 'Predictors of pronunciation accuracy in second language learning', *Language Learning*, 26, 2, 233–53.

Swain M. (1985), 'Communicative competence: some roles of comprehensible input and comprehensible output in its development', In Gass and Madden (eds.) (1985).

—— and Burnaby B. (1976), 'Personality characteristics and second language learning in young children', *Working Papers on Bilingualism*, 11, 115–28.

Symonds P.M. (1930), *Foreign Language Prognosis Test*, New York: Teachers College, Bureau of Publications.

Tarone E. (1983), 'On the variability of interlanguage systems', *Applied Linguistics*, 4, 2, 142–63.

—— (1988), *Variation in Interlanguage*, London: Edward Arnold.

Taylor J.A. (1953), 'A personality scale of manifest anxiety', *Journal of Abnormal and Social Psychology*, 48, 285–90.

Thurstone L.L. and Thurstone T.G. (1965), *Primary Mental Abilities Test*, (Rev. 1962), Chicago: Science Research Associates.

Tikunoff W.J. (1985), *Developing student functional proficiency for LEP students*, San Francisco: Center for Interactive Research and Development.

Tizard B. and Hughes M. (1984), *Young children learning*, London: Fontana.

Tucker G.R., Hamayan E., and Genessee F.H. (1976), 'Affective cognitive, and social factors in second language acquisition', *Canadian Modern Language Review*, 32, 214–26.

Upshur J.A., Acton W., Arthur B., and Guiora A. (1978), 'Causation or correlation: A reply to Oller and Perkins', *Language Learning*, 28, 2, 99–104.

Vernon P. (1961), *The Structure of Human Abilities*, London: Methuen.

Vollmer H. and Sang F. (1983), 'Competing hypotheses about second language ability: a plea for caution', In Oller (1983).

Wankowski J. (1973), *Temperament, Motivation, and Academic Achievement*, Birmingham: University of Birmingham Educational Counselling Unit.

Wells C.G. (1981), *Learning Through Interaction*, Cambridge University Press.

—— (1985), *Language Development in the Pre-School Years*, Cambridge University Press.

—— (1986), 'Variation in child language', In Fletcher P. and Garman T. (eds.) *Language Acquisition*, (2nd edn) Cambridge University Press.

Wells W., Wesche M., and Sarrazin G. (1982), *Test d'Aptitude aux Langues Vivantes* (adapted from Carroll and Sapon (1959)), Montreal: Institute for Psychological Research.

Wells W. (ed.) (1983), *Test d'Aptitude aux Langues Vivantes*, Ottawa: Student Services Division, Language Training Branch, Public Service Commission of Canada.

Wenden A. (1983), 'The process of intervention', *Language Learning*, 33, 1, 103–21.

—— (1986), 'What do second language learners know about their language learning?: A second look at retrospective accounts', *Applied Linguistics*, 7, 2, 186–.

—— (1987a), 'How to be a successful language learner: Insights and prescriptions from L2 learners', In Wenden and Rubin (eds.) (1987).

—— (1987b), 'Incorporating learner training in the classroom', In Wenden and Rubin (eds.) (1987).

—— and Rubin J. (1987), *Learner Strategies in Language Learning*, Englewood Cliffs, NJ: Prentice-Hall.

Wesche M.B. (1981), 'Language aptitude measures in streaming, matching students with methods, and diagnosis of learning problems', In Diller (ed.) (1981).

——, Edwards H., and Wells W. (1982) 'Foreign language aptitude and intelligence', *Applied Psycholinguistics*, 3, 127–40.

—— and Schniederman E.I. (nd) 'Language lateralisation, language aptitude, and cognitive style in second language learning', University of Ottawa.

Wickelgren W. (1979), *Cognitive psychology*, Englewood Cliffs, NJ: Prentice-Hall.

Widdowson H.G. (1983) *Learner purpose and language use*, Oxford University Press.

Wishart D. (1978), *CLUSTAN: User Manual*, Program Library Unit, Edinburgh University.

Witkin H.A. (1962), *Psychological Differentiation*, New York: Wiley.

——, Oltman P.K., Raskin E., and Karp S.A. (1971), *A Manual for the Embedded Figures Test*, Palo Alto, Cal. California Consulting Psychology Press.

——, Goodenough D. and Oltman P. (1979), 'Psychological differentiation: Current status', *Journal of Personality and Social Psychology*, 37, 1127–45.

Wong-Fillmore L. (1976), *The second time around: Cognitive and social strategies in second language acquisition*, Unpublished Ph.D. dissertation, Stanford University.

—— (1979), 'Individual differences in second language acquisition', In Fillmore C.J., Wang W-S.Y., and Kempler D. (eds.) *Individual differences in language ability and language behaviour*, New York: Academic Press.

—— (1982), 'The language learner as an individual: Implications of research on individual differences for the ESL teacher', In Clark M. and Handscombe J. (eds.) *On TESOL '82*, Washington, DC: TESOL.

—— (1985), 'Second language learning in children: A proposed model', In Eshch R. and Provinzano J. (eds.), *Issues in English Language Development*, National Clearinghouse for Bilingual Education, Rosslyn, Virginia.

—— and others (1986), *Learning English through Bilingual Instruction: Final Report*, Washington, DC: National Institute of Education, (Available as ED 259579).

Woods A., Fletcher P., and Hughes A. (1986), *Statistics in language studies*, Cambridge University Press.

Yemi-Komshian G. (1965), *Training procedures for developing auditory perception skills in the sound system of a foreign language*, Unpublished Ph.D. dissertation, McGill University.

Zampogna J., Gentile R.J., Papalia A., and Gordon R. (1976), 'Relationships between learning styles and learning environments in selected secondary modern language classrooms', *Modern Language Journal*, 60, 443–8.

Index

Subject Index

Name index